I0840857

Cuts through coaching jargon, simplifies the journey and offers a lived personal and practical approach to the dance of coaching. I connected with this in a different way from any other coaching books.

Lewis Moody, Performance Coach, former England Rugby Captain

This is a must read. The lessons learned in this book will stick with me throughout my coaching career, and I thank you for the amazing insights.

Jane Hanson, Emmy award-winning television journalist and coach

This book made me pause, ponder, smile, reflect, take courage. The authors offer a synthesis of becoming not only a coach, but a grounded and wise human. Step by step, they create a safe space for personal reflection and growth, for recognition of our strengths and our weaknesses as humans and as facilitators. This is a book that feels more like a personal encounter, a conversation with a coach whose interest is in the reader flourishing. This isn't just a book about coaching, it's a book about how to live.

Dr Kathryn Mannix, author of *Listen*

A refreshing contribution to the field of coaching. It offers deep wisdom in rare bite-size, easily digestible nuggets. It peels back the layers and courageously interconnects our core humanity to coaching. It emphasizes the power of true silence and eloquently elaborates the true meaning of shared power and partnership. I would highly recommend the book to anyone seeking a deeper, more intimate and authentic connection with oneself and others.

Shruti Sonathlia MCC, recipient of the ICF Young Leader Award 2022 and Executive Coach

Artful coaching is not about DOING better techniques. It is about BEING more human. *The Human Behind the Coach* is a definitive guide for who we need to become in order to demonstrate greater ease, flow, confidence and deep partnership in our coaching. This is a personal growth guidebook for anyone who wants to be a transformative presence in the world.

Fran Fisher MCC, author of *Calling Forth Greatness*

Coaching is at its best when the coach can navigate the full breadth of their humanity in service of their clients. This book gives you the keys for how to do that.

Lori Shook MCC, author of *Coaches Going Corporate*

In this remarkable work, the authors skilfully weave together personal anecdotes, insightful reflections and thought-provoking wisdom to delve into the depths of what it truly means to be human. A poignant reminder for coaches to do their own work within – otherwise they will never be able to go deep with their clients. Prepare to be moved, inspired and forever changed by this transformative literary masterpiece.

Dr Don Eisenhauer, Founder of Coaching at End of Life

An invaluable resource for coaches seeking to enhance their coaching skills. *The Human Behind the Coach* is a compelling invitation to join the dance of masterful coaching by becoming more mindful and intentional within the coaching space.

Lyssa deHart, LICSW, MCC, BCC, author of *StoryJacking* and *The Reflective Coach*

Whether you are starting out as a coach or are a seasoned practitioner, this book forms an excellent and very timely guide to becoming an 'artful' rather than a 'masterful' coach. Essential reading for all coaches and supervisors in professional relational work.

Fiona Adamson, author and award-winning supervisor, Co-Founder of CSA

Whether you coach teams or individuals, this book is bound to contribute to your effectiveness by demonstrating how a true coaching mindset relies above all on a series of universal human qualities that can and must be developed. It shows you how to avoid letting the professional in you mask the human in you, reminding you that – in essence – you are already enough and showing you the way to become a more transformative practitioner by letting go. A book that will make you a better coach – and quite possibly a better human.

Allard de Jong (Director) and Georgina Woudstra (Founder), Team Coaching Studio

Humanity not pedigree in coaching. This is a wonderful contribution to the coaching profession focusing on the beauty and magic of humanity in coaching. Claire and Lucia encourage coaches to look further than the rules to focus on the human element. Drawing on spirituality, psychology and personal wisdom to inform a coach's way of being makes this a must read.

Karen Foy, Programme Director Professional Certificate in Executive Coaching, Henley Business School

Claire and Lucia have categorically laid to rest the concern that coaches would be made redundant by technology, especially artificial intelligence. *The Human Behind the Coach* is central in effecting transformative conversations that would change lives for the better. While tools and techniques are important to our trade, it is our humanity that enables transformational coaching sessions.

Ivan Yong Wei Kit, Adjunct Professor, coach and mentor, Hong Kong

I wish I'd had this book at my elbow earlier in my coaching career. Wisdom pours from every page.

Katharine St John-Brooks, author of *Internal Coaching: The Inside Story*

This is a book with a unique and vital perspective. It's looking inside the coach at their humaneness – from within and between the coach and other humans. It profoundly explores aspects rarely or too lightly touched on in other books. But these are the essence of being a great coach, for example, navigating silence, humility, partnership and trust. Two master coaches freely share their craft secrets clearly and powerfully, all focused on becoming a more aware human and, of course, a better coach.

Bob Galen, Principal Coach at Agile Moose

This book is a true gift to our coaching profession. I have so appreciated and enjoyed reading the words of Claire and Lucia with their wisdom, deep experience, inspiration and reflection. The book de-mystifies the journey towards mastery and provides some tangible focus areas for coaches when thinking about their development. It will be a go-to resource for me as a mentor partnering with my coach mentees on their journey of discovery.

Anna Inama ICF MCC coach, mentor and team coach

Claire and Lucia bring their wealth of experience as coaches to explore the techniques and the human states that lie at the heart of being an artful coach. They offer really practical ways for coaches to engage with the humanity within all coaching relationships and in doing so hone their craft. This book is stacked full of practices, questions and examples of how to continue to grow as a coach, offered in a highly accessible way, by two coaches at the top of their game. A must read for coaches wanting to deepen their practice at any stage of their development.

Becky Hall, coach and author of *The Art of Enough: 7 Ways to Build a Balanced Life and a Flourishing World*

A unique and timely blend of voices. In addition to the voices of Claire and Lucia, the reader is introduced to the insights and commentary of countless artful coaches and a diverse group of influential thinkers. The result is a robust, compelling and unique presentation of artful coaching.

Dr J. Val Hastings MCC, President and Founder of Coaching4Today'sLeaders

The Human Behind the Coach is not only for coaches but for anyone who wants to engage with others in a more meaningful way. With clear, effective and actionable steps, Claire and Lucia demystify the coaching process, distilling it down to the most simple and effective structure and strategies. This book will not just make you a better coach, but a better human.

Jamie Fiore Higgins, coach, speaker and author of *Bully Market, My Story of Money and Misogyny at Goldman Sachs*

THE HUMAN BEHIND THE COACH

How great coaches transform themselves first

CLAIRE PEDRICK MCC

LUCIA BALDELLI MCC

First published in Great Britain by Practical Inspiration Publishing, 2023

ISBN   9781788604567 (print)
       9781788604581 (epub)
       9781788604574 (mobi)

Want to bulk-buy copies of this book for your team and colleagues? We can customize the content and co-brand *The Human Behind the Coach* to suit your business's needs.

Please email info@practicalinspiration.com for more details.

DEDICATION

This book is dedicated to

Claire's dad Michael and her husband Mike, and
Lucia's husband Marco

who have inspired and supported us to be better humans

TABLE OF CONTENTS

FOREWORD

One of the things that distinguishes a human coach from an artificially intelligent (AI) robot is our humanity. Yet, coach education predominantly focuses on equipping coaches with processes and models, which an AI robot can replicate with relative ease. In my own coaching practice, we saw the impact of this in a series of coach assessment centres more than a decade ago. Almost all the executive coaches putting themselves forward had certificates to prove that they had achieved at least a basic level of competence in administering a coaching process, such as GROW. Yet, more than half of them failed to create a learning environment where the client could reflect. The model was driving the coaching; to the extent that it appeared at times to be robotic.

Of course, coaches need to have some understanding of processes and models, to structure meaningful, insight-provoking conversations, and to be a skeleton on which to hang their reflections. But when processes and models become substitutes for presence and being, they lead to sterile, predictable conversations. The coach's agenda unconsciously takes precedence over the client's – for example, in aiming to find a resolution to a problem within the coaching conversation, rather than helping the client evolve in their thinking, so they can continue to reflect and come to their own conclusions, in their own time and in their own way.

Our research into coach maturity has themes emerge that are strongly parallel to those that you will see in the following pages. Among them are:

- *The critical importance of reflection*, in multiple forms, including personal contemplation and effective use of supervision.
- *Doing less to achieve more.* For example, coaches learned to give up dependence on SMART goals or knowing where the conversation was going.
- *Use of self.* These coaches had sufficient self-awareness that, by letting go of processes, they gave full rein to their intuition and the Gestalt of the moment. They use their wisdom and experience (as a coach, as a professional and as a human being) as a resource to create stronger rapport, to generate more insightful and original questions and to offer appropriate context, where it helped the client's thinking. In many ways, they became more like mentors (in the original, wisdom-oriented meaning of the word).

Another finding of our research that I see strongly demonstrated in this book is an understanding that sometimes borders on wonder at what it means to be a complete human being, secure in the knowledge that they and their clients are all works in progress. I find here a remarkable parallel between what happens to children in our standard educational systems and what happens to coaches within standard coach education. In both cases, the system works to drum the sense of wonder out of them – it just happens earlier for coaches. Becoming a mature human being and becoming a mature coach both require us to rediscover our sense of curious wonderment, at our clients, at ourselves and at the world around us. This book will help coaches along that journey of rediscovery!

David Clutterbuck

ACKNOWLEDGEMENTS

We are grateful to everyone who has affirmed that coaching is about simplicity and humanity and who has encouraged us to keep writing. We thank the provocateurs who ask questions that get us thinking, through conversations, mentoring and supervision groups, training, webinars and LinkedIn. We appreciate the coaches who have shown us how to communicate the dance and the music of our work. Finally, we would like to thank every person we have coached, supervised or mentored – each of you has been our teacher.

Our special thanks go to Alison Jones and the team at Practical Inspiration Publishing, Fiona Adamson, Lucy Bolster, Alistair Bradley, Eve Burt, Holly Crane, Gary Crotaz, Jo Guz, Sara Hodge, ICF Israel Chapter, Jose Knowles, Mike Leigh, Natalie Marguet, Stuart Reid, Victoria Saint, Katharine St John-Brooks, Catherine St John Smith, Kim Witten (for the insights on linguistics and embodied cognition) and Beatrice Zornek.

We would also like to thank our teams for their prompt and precious input when all of this was still quite messy (Peronel Barnes, Ruth Bennett, Su Blanch, Karen Bruns, Vanessa Callis, Zoe Dickinson, Alan Gyle, Rebi Hedger (who helped us find the title), Chester Jackson, Alexandru Popa-Antohi, Mike Williams), our many endorsers and beta readers for the insightful feedback and the kind words about our work, and our families for their support and patience when this book prevented us from spending more time with them.

INTRODUCTION: WHERE DID OUR HUMANITY GO?

We are human people. Claire is from the UK and Lucia is Italian. When we aren't living our home lives with friends and family, we are coaches. The lessons we have learned through our everyday lives have been a significant part of our development. We bring learning from many thousands of hours of our own coaching conversations and from the conversations we have listened to with those we train, supervise and mentor. We have learned from many different training programmes, mentors and supervisors of our own.[1] The personal and professional have shaped our thinking and the ideas behind this book. We will tell you some of our stories here.

Our speech and how it sounds is informed by the cultures we come from and inhabit. We're influenced by our families of origin, where we have been educated, where we have lived and worked, and much more. We speak from those places; they are our identities. In your places, the sounds of conversation may be different from ours. Even when we share colour, identity features such as gender, race, sexual orientation, work experience and life experience, we also share differences. We come from diverse, beautiful, multi-faceted cultures. We invite you to make what is written here your own as you explore the impact of words and sounds in your own conversations.

---

[1] Come and visit us on LinkedIn to see our qualifications and training. We would love to hear from you and see how we could work together. #Claire Pedrick MCC and #Lucia Baldelli MCC

We met online in early 2021 during lockdown. It became clear that the work we were doing together could become a book. What you are reading has been co-created from ideas that emerged over many conversations. We met face to face for the first time at a writing retreat in Italy to complete the final manuscript. The conversation continues as we develop a live training programme for people who would like to join in this exploration with us.

The book we started to write was called *Growing into Mastery*. The initial idea was to explore the shifts coaches need to make as they aspire to mastery. Our readers might have been people interested in achieving the Master Certified Coach (MCC) credential with the International Coaching Federation (ICF). Other people might have read it for their professional development and to better serve those who they coach.

Lucia wrote this as we began:

There are quite a few mindset shifts that have to happen in order to be a masterful coach. These are magic moments when you learn something and suddenly realize how you could be more effective in service of your client's learning. They happened to me in different ways: while I was coaching, teaching classes to my students, listening to masterclasses, talking to my mentor and supervisor and reading books. I like to consider them little milestones because they mark the path of incredible growth. They build on the 'core qualities' that are essential for each specific competency and allow you to be in true partnership with your client throughout the conversation. I would like to talk about how we bring those qualities into our work.

This was the moment when our initial idea changed. As we listened to each other, and to other coaches, we recognized that the word mastery can evoke mixed feelings. Mastery is about doing great work. But many coaches are put off from doing deeper development when they feel it is about ticking boxes, gaining power, othering or making sure they hit markers even when they are not needed in the room.

Both of us are ICF Master Certified Coaches and choose to work with people like you, who aspire to be ever better at their craft. We recognize that wisdom from life, coach training and experience come together as coaches develop. We have chosen to talk about **growing**, **experienced** and **artful** as stages of a coach's development. These are not necessarily connected to the length of time someone has been coaching. You won't hear about mastery from us again – this book is about artfulness! More than two years later, our question has become:

What needs to change for us on the inside to be able to demonstrate ease and partnership in coaching?

A lot has been written about how to do coaching. Artful coaching is not about doing more or better, nor about more or slicker techniques. It is about being more human: moving from thinking about skillset and toolset to life-set and mindset. Developing on the inside is the real work.

Coaches facilitate conversations. Millionaires who have made their money from coaching might attribute the greatness of their conversations to their charisma more than their technique, but competence is a prerequisite to genuine self-confidence that enables you to trust yourself and the process. You finally come to believe that, no matter what happens in the room, it is going to be OK. When you listen to many professional bodies in coaching, it feels like it is the competencies that matter. Competencies can feel like rules. Your humanity shows up in the flow of the conversation and the connection you make together.

OPENING UP THE CONVERSATION

Author Simon Walker talks about how leaders are backstage and front stage.[2] So are coaches. We can't invest all of our energy and resources in the technical skill for the front stage of the coaching session without making sure that we're also paying attention to our backstage humanity.

We notice a common theme across the coaches we work with, whatever their accreditation or training: the focus is louder on technical skill than humanity. Claire spoke to John Blakey at *The Coaching Inn* podcast. John and Ian Day wrote *Challenging Coaching* in 2012 to open up conversation about challenge because coaching appeared to be primarily about individual development through building support, trust and rapport. It is our hope that this book will open up the conversation about humanity. As an industry, how can we hold onto our professional standards and bring in more of our humanity? Since we released the title of this book, we have been overwhelmed with feedback that agrees it is time to talk about being human in coaching.

WHAT WE ARE LEARNING

The writing process has been a conversation – between us and with others. The deepest insight for us came when we started to explore the human qualities that coaches demonstrate in the room to turn what looks, on a transcript, like a word-perfect conversation into artful coaching. We looked at many qualities including wisdom and curiosity. In the end, we picked the six that we think have the greatest impact:

- Silence
- Control and not knowing
- Humility
- Vulnerability

---

[2] Walker (2010)

- Distance
- Courage and insight

We explore these in Part I, *Humanity within*. They can be observed in the partnership, the words, the music and the dance of the conversation.

In Part II, *Humanity between*, we explore what the development from a great technical coach to an artful one looks like, sounds like and feels like.

No one ever sets out with the intention of not being human, but when we feel a bit overwhelmed about getting coaching right, and listening properly, our humanity can disappear behind the work we are doing. When we show our human side, we allow the other person to show theirs. Shaun Lambert, who studies mindfullness (*sic*), says that 'our role can take over – we have to show with humility that we are human beings.'[3]

Since *Simplifying Coaching* was published in 2020, coaches from across the world have messaged to say how useful it has been to understand, more simply, how to create a container to have a conversation that is transformational – where someone has new insights into their own stuff that move them forward.[4] Two themes have stood out:

- Coaches value a book written by practitioners for practitioners that is easy to understand.
- Knowing how to simplify coaching, wanting to do it and actually being able to do it are not the same things.

The Human Behind the Coach is the prequel. What needs to change in us so that our coaching can become simpler and more transformational?

____

[3] Lambert (2014)

[4] Pedrick (2020)

As we have co-created the book, there have been a number of times when we have talked about the connection between emotion, coaching and neuroscience. We have chosen not to reference it because there are others who are far more skilled at explaining it than we are. When you make the connection, which we are sure you will, we invite you to dig deeper into resources from neuroscience specialists like Amy Brann and David Rock in the Bibliography.

Before we dive in, let's clarify some of the words that you will find throughout the book:

- We work with human people. We choose to call them *thinkers*.[5]
- Coaching conversations have a beginning, a middle and an end. We call this arc *the coaching container*.
- *Transformation*, for us, is when people have new insights that will make a difference in a sustainable way.
- *Flow*. Coach Alistair Bradley describes relational flow in coaching when:

> time seems to stand still, I am completely absorbed in what I am doing, and everything flows beautifully and effortlessly in the service of my client. I am left feeling fulfilled, knowing I was at my best and believing I made a difference.[6]

Flow demonstrates ease for the coach and the thinker. It comes when you let go of your attachment to asking exactly the right question in exactly the right way. Alistair defines relational flow as 'the deep, human and transformational connection between coach and client'.[7] Your work cannot flow in partnership when you are trying to do too much, because you interrupt their flow and forward movement.

---

[5] Ibid

[6] Bradley (2022)

[7] Ibid

In Part II we will talk about some of the ways to see and hear flow in the dance, the words and the music of the conversation.

Team coach director Allard de Jong adapted the words from a poem by John O'Donohue to create a beautiful aspiration for coaching: 'I would love to [coach] like a river flows, carried by the surprise of its own unfolding.'[8]

Coaching is like sewing. Each intervention is a stitch that seamlessly picks up from the last. Each intervention is not a new and disconnected question, it gently moves the conversation forward, connecting back to their previous answer.

Flow comes when you stop getting in the way right from the beginning of the conversation. *Rightsizing* is the way you agree together, in partnership:[9]

- What are we doing today?
- How are we going to do it?
- How will we know we have done it?

At the beginning, you are in flow when you weave your questions about what you are doing into what they have said as your question builds from their answer:

something about stress, so which bit of that is useful to work on today?

In the middle of the conversation, you are in flow when you do the least you need to do to keep them moving without it being awkward for them:

so...?

---

[8] O'Donohue (2001)

[9] Pedrick (2020)

At the end, flow might sound like speeding up as you both increase energy to get to action and beyond:

and now you know that...?

You may think that rightsizing is prescriptive, and yet Alistair Bradley observes that without any framework, you can lead the thinker into a sea of possibility and possibly lostness.[10] With too much framework they can experience the conversation as stilted. He describes four types of coaching:

- *Passive*: We go where we like (not driven).
- *Dialogue*: A purposeful conversation in partnership (partnership driven).
- *Performance*: I use the tools and techniques which I like (tool driven).
- *Solo performance*: This is my show (ego driven).

ICF talk about mastery being demonstrated 'completely, effortlessly and consistently in response to what the client presents.'[11] What distinguishes **the artful coach** is less eager, less ego; more ease, more depth. Artful coaching happens when you are in dialogue. In partnership. In flow.

---

[10] Bradley (2022)

[11] ICF MCC bars

HOW TO USE THIS BOOK

The Human Behind the Coach is about *how to be a coach.*

It is for humans who want to have more impactful one-to-one conversations at work and outside of work: people who might be coaches, counsellors, therapists, psychologists, supervisors, people managers, leaders at all levels, human resource (HR) professionals, team leaders, agile coaches, facilitators, teachers and more.

This book is for practitioners who want to learn to work better in partnership with ease and to create more flow in your conversations; for those who want to stop ticking boxes, embrace artful coaching and show up as their best self, inside and outside the room.

We hope that we will spark thoughts and insights in you as you make this your own. There are opportunities to engage in reflections and exercises throughout the book. Please consider them as offers to try, not rules to follow.

Here are the different types of activities that you will find:

- **Questions to think about.** Questions for individual reflection that connect you to the topic we are about to discuss or invite you to think further to bring what you have just read to your own context to make your own meaning.

- **Look for this**. Things to look for as you reflect on your practice to link what you have learned in each chapter. You might choose to:
  - reflect on a recent session, if you are away from your computer;
  - watch a recording of your coaching.

- **Try this**. Low-risk experiments that you can try immediately, even with people you are coaching. If you read fast, please don't apply all the learning in your next session!

- **Try this with a peer coach**. Experiments that we suggest you try with a peer to gain some confidence, before you use them in a coaching room – that isn't the place for too much experimentation!

- **Explore** how to watch recordings in Chapter 12 where you will find details about how to do recordings, and more ideas of what else to look for.

If you enjoy this and would like to engage in further learning with us, then please download our free workbook (see www.thehumanbehindthecoach.com), which contains exercises from this book and more.

PART 1
HUMANITY WITHIN

Six human qualities underpin artful coaching:

- Silence
- Control and not knowing
- Humility
- Vulnerability
- Distance
- Courage and insight

If you want to dig deeper into this work, self-reflection and supervision are useful places to explore more.

CHAPTER 1
SILENCE

There are more than 20,000 business books on Amazon about asking questions, more than 40,000 about coaching and fewer than 1,000 about silence. And yet 'silence is where the real work happens,' says palliative care doctor and author Kathryn Mannix.[1] If we believe this, why do we talk so much?

If the art of coaching is to do the least amount of work in service of the thinker doing great thinking so that they get new insights, we need to leave them enough space to do that. Much of their new insight will emerge in their silence. 'The thinker does not have to talk,' says author Nancy Kline. 'They can, if they choose, be silent the entire time. Their job is to think. Often the most important insights arise in the thinker's silence, aided by the partner's silence,' she adds.[2] Unless our silence strategy is to cover our mouths with duct tape, developing our capacity to be silent on the outside requires us to start by engaging our own feelings and attitudes about being silent on the inside.

Coaching is a dialogue that we facilitate. The most significant part of the dialogue is the conversation this unique individual has with themselves. 'When you hear a word like dialogue you probably think of conversation with others but, as strange as it may sound, dialogue begins with yourself,' says leadership educator William Isaacs.[3] The

---

[1] Mannix (2021)
[2] Kline (2020)
[3] Isaacs (1999)

journey to becoming a better coach does not begin with reading another book or going on another course. It begins with you.

WHY SILENCE MATTERS

Do you remember talking through a challenge and, by just talking, felt better or had new insights? Kathryn Mannix explains that 'sharing our difficulties is one of the keys to surviving them without becoming completely broken.'[4] As we share facts and emotions, we gain new clarity. We get insights about our experiences and understand the way forward. This can happen even when our listener is a silent partner offering neither question nor comment. We simply need someone to be there and bear witness as we go deeper to explore what is going on.

Empathy is essential for great listening and is a prerequisite for silence to be genuine and not forced. A great listener co-creates and holds space. This is holy ground. Any sense of judging or minimizing the challenge can quickly shut down a conversation. Silence creates the conditions for generative processing where people can make sense of their own experience. Great listeners are comfortable with whatever emotions show up – whether invited or not. They stay with the thinker and sit with the emotions in silence, kindly accept them, acknowledge them if appropriate and give the thinker autonomy to decide whether they need any attention in this conversation.

ATTITUDES TO SILENCE

We come from Italy and the UK. Our countries have very different attitudes to silence. Individuals differ too. Some love silence, others will avoid it at any price. Some people like interrupting others or building hypotheses that are useful if we are having an argument or solving a problem. It also means we are having a conversation on our own instead of listening fully to another. Bringing genuine silence into a conversation can be difficult when we are busy making

---

[4] Mannix (2020)

sense of their world through the lenses of our own opinions, ideas, experiences and emotions. It's messy and confusing and it makes it very hard to see, hear or sense what the other person is saying.

Any transformational conversation requires us to engage in a different way. We need silence. 'I've begun to realize that you can listen to silence and learn from it. It has a quality and a dimension all its own,' writes novelist Chaim Potok.[5] In the thinker's silence, there is much to notice. We hear (sighs, shifts of energy), we see (eyes looking away, body movements) and we sense (discomfort, hesitation). Being silent on the outside by not talking is a start. Just because we aren't making a noise does not mean that we are being silent.

Greek philosopher Plutarch said that 'silence at the proper season is wisdom, and better than any speech.' While we hold on to a belief that our words add value, silence will evoke fear in us. The value of the work we do together is not about what the thinker hears us say. It is about what happens in them and what happens in the space between us. The question we ask ourselves all the time is: *What is the least I need to do today for this person to feel seen and heard and have new insights into their own stuff?* This is a head shift for coaches who are collectors of shiny tools and techniques and prepare for a session by thinking about all the amazing things they could do together. When your toolkit is overflowing, there won't be much space for silence. Silence is useful when you give yourself permission to use it.

QUESTIONS TO THINK ABOUT

- What's your attitude to silence?
- What makes silence challenging for you?
- What would you like to be different about the way you use silence?

---

[5] Potok (2009)

BEING SILENT ON THE INSIDE

'Listening,' says Isaacs, 'requires us to develop an "inner silence".'[6] This is where we need to do our own work. While we are silently talking to ourselves, framing questions, thinking of tools or solutions, or deciding what to have for dinner, we are not silent. Even for a skilled multi-tasker some attention is being diverted from being present for the thinker. 'Listening requires we not only hear the words but also embrace, accept and gradually let go of our own inner clambering.'[7] This capacity to be present and to be silent inside is as important as the actual work of listening. The person you are with may be processing and moving forwards. They will sense when you are thinking inside and might pause to hear what you have to say.

The volume and distraction of what's going on inside our heads can vary. Some have loud inner voices. Others are naturally quiet. The first step to get better at silence is to stop making a noise. The next step is our internal work to develop what Isaacs calls 'a simple but profound capacity to listen.'[8] This is different for everyone. We may be skilled at listening or we may have been coaching for many years and recognize that there is still work to be done here. We can't have meaningful and impactful conversations until we have the capacity to be present. Our overthinking facilitates under-thinking in others. What would it be like if we only spoke when what we are about to say is more useful than the silence? Our ideas, insights, distractions and inner chatter may not be what this person needs right now.

Silence requires humility. What we see, hear and sense, and then what we say and do are only part of the process of the conversation. We are not single-handedly responsible for it all, and definitely not the star of the show. Nancy Kline describes much of the training for professional listeners, including coaches, as a place where 'the instruction is effectively... how to insert, how to tailgate, how to

---

[6] Isaacs (1999)

[7] Ibid

[8] Ibid

justify the populating of silence with our own view.'[9] None of that is silence.

Claire once spent a few days walking in the desert. It was silent. No sound. Being completely silent on the inside would require absolutely no sound and chatter in our heads. Given that we are human people, that may well be unattainable. A next step to engage with silence could be to ask ourselves what we need to do or stop doing to be able to listen to our internal voice less. Until we learn to turn down the volume on our own stuff a bit, it is difficult to hold silence with someone else. When we can quieten the noise, we are more able to listen to what we see or hear or sense in our companion. 'And when we are in relational flow, our internal chatter stops.'[10]

Isaacs describes inner silence as a 'state into which one can let go', rather than a place where we suppress ourselves.'[11] There are many ways to cultivate inner silence and pay more attention: meditation, mindfulness, prayer or a pragmatic view of letting go. We can learn to notice what we feel in our body, our emotions, the voices speaking inside our heads and the ones that are marginalized. Untamed, all these affect the way we come across to others.

When we understand the value of silence, we welcome whatever comes up for the thinker, so they can make sense of it too. Holding silence together can push our dialogue to a deeper level and enable them to have greater discovery.

ARRIVING STILL

It is useful to *arrive still* in your mind, so that you can focus entirely on what is happening to the person in front of you and avoid being distracted by what you were thinking or doing just before the session. How can you both arrive still? The preparation you do to arrive in each and every conversation is as important as any coaching book or technique you might read.

---

[9] Kline (2020)

[10] Bradley (2022)

[11] Isaacs (1999)

What happens when the thinker arrives in a hurry, or late, or with some unfinished business? Unless you address it at the start, you will be using the conversation to slow them down before you can get in flow. They have to shut down their inner noise, just like you do. It allows them to be focused on what they want out of your time together and be less distracted.

When the thinker arrives overwhelmed, you can have a conversation about what will be useful for them to arrive still. It could be a breathing exercise, a minute of silence, a coffee break or decompressing for a contained amount of time. You ask. They choose. Making the time at the start will allow you both to make the rest of the conversation the right size for the day's session.[12]

Most of the progress happens in between sessions, but only if thinkers make time to reflect and move forward. Invite them to plan how they will make time and create the silent space for that reflection on their own.

TRY THIS

Here are a few practices that might help. And you will have your own.

- Turn down the volume on the voice in your head before you arrive in the room. Some coaches meditate, read their notes or simply get a coffee. It doesn't really matter as long as it helps to arrive still.
- Ask yourself: *Am I in a good place to have this conversation?* Notice your own thoughts and feelings, so that you can become aware of your own needs – and find a safe place to park them before the session.
- Practise focusing your attention in the present moment, non-judgmentally, with curiosity and kindness.

---

[12] Pedrick (2020)

FORGETTING

We can struggle with being quieter on the inside because we respond to others based on how we interpret what they are saying, and what is happening in us as they speak. We make connections with our own story, or with a story we heard from someone else. When we try to solve their problem, our stop-trying-to-solve-their-problem voice has a sound of its own. We listen simply so that they can hear themselves. Isaacs recommends developing a habit of 'self-forgetting' to create a space where listening can occur.[13] Forgetting is an important quality. Like a non-stick cooking pan, a Teflon memory means that what we hear doesn't need to stick with us. We can stop listening to remember. They will remember what matters. Our role is to be attentive and present enough for our companion to do some great work. It is not to do it for them. Nor to do it for them in our head while pretending we are being silent and fully listening! We are there to enable them to make their own meaning from what they hear themselves saying. We can never make meaning for them. We are not the expert in the room. Our role is to co-facilitate their thinking with them.[14]

The active part of active listening is about silence – turning down the noise of our own ego, thoughts, memories, opinions, experience, and turning up our curiosity about what is happening in the person in front of us. As we learn to be fully present and in tune with the people we work with, we might realize that the initial exhaustion of a coaching session comes from the effort required to quiet our inner dialogue. We cannot be present and listen until we can hold silence inside ourselves.

Professor Jon Kabat-Zinn, founder of the Center for Mindfulness in Medicine, Health Care and Society in Massachusetts, describes the value of paying complete attention to what is going on moment-to-moment in an open and non-judgemental way. This is his definition of mindfulness. Isn't this exactly what we need in coaching? To have conversations that allow us to be fully aware of the here-and-now

---

[13] Isaacs (1999)

[14] Pedrick (2020)

experience of the thinker and what's happening between us, so that we can welcome whatever comes with kindness, empathy and acceptance. We can only have these conversations and really listen when we have learned to turn down the volume on the noise in our head. This is why inner silence matters.

WHAT SILENCE FEELS LIKE

Some people love silence. Others will do everything they can to fill it. A research project from the University of Groningen in the Netherlands explored cultural attitudes to silence. 'When a silence in conversation stretched to four seconds, people [Dutch and English] started to feel unsettled. A separate study of business meetings discovered that Japanese people were happy with silences of 8.2 seconds.'[15] Coaching will often have much longer silences.

Silence can be generated by either of us, or co-created. Sometimes it is generative and useful and keeps the conversation in flow, and sometimes it is awkward for one or both of us. We need to work out together what will serve the thinker. This comes from watching, checking in and being aware of our preference and that it might not serve our work.

Our attitudes impact how we manage silence. When you sense that nothing is happening and that they are looking at you to 'get them out of here', how do you feel? If you're being paid to be here in this dialogue, you may feel awkward because you feel you should know what to do. Your inner voice starts asking you questions:

- Am I adding enough value?
- Was this my fault?
- Maybe I should just tell them what I think they should do?
- Why won't they say something?!

While you have that much noise, you can't fully listen.

---

15 Morrison (2017)

QUESTIONS TO THINK ABOUT

- What noises does your inner voice make?
- What strategies do you use to lower the volume?
- What else could help you going forward?

WHAT'S HAPPENING WHEN THEY ARE SILENT

Let's not make assumptions about how people use silence. Here are six of our thoughts about what might be happening when it's quiet.

1. They are being silent inside and inviting you to keep them company while they hold it

Claire worked with someone who goes silent when an insight is forming. She emerges from the silence in about the same place. She was seeing how it fitted. She hasn't moved forward, but she has gone deeper.

Others will use silence to think and make leaps forward. When they emerge, they will be in a completely different place. Lucia worked with a man who connected with himself deeply and in silence: he needed a space to listen to his body and emotions to make meaning. Their sessions had long pauses when Lucia simply bore witness while he was exploring. Being there, watching and waiting was the best work she could do.

How much silence we use will depend on how much they can tolerate – some thinkers need more from us, others need less. Rather than thinking what to do next, we sense this from the dance between us. In silence, check in non-verbally and often.

2. They are busy thinking

This is generative silence. The conversation is in flow. They are moving. We need to be quiet on the inside or we won't notice where to come in and what will be needed when we do. Try watching them like you are watching a compelling film.

The thinker needs to be our focus, not our thoughts. 'A person's generative attention loses its power the very second it wavers. Attention like this has to be continuous,' says Nancy Kline.[16] As we observe experienced coaches who are working on the art of doing less, we notice that even a click as you swallow a question after half a syllable is enough to invite the thinker to listen to you rather than to themselves. You can accidentally end the silence by moving, leaning in or taking a breath as you prepare to speak – not only when you ask a question or make an observation.

Nancy Kline describes breaking the silence as silently saying:

> Stop! Look at me. I know better than you what you need now. You need me to speak. I don't care where you would have gone in your thinking just then. I do not care... I care that you recognize my value to you because of what I am saying right now.[17]

They will tell you when they need you – with their eyes, their words or their bodies. They will only remain in flow after the silence is over if you were fully present while they were busy. To stay in connection, you will need to look, listen and sense. If you start planning what to ask or do next during the silence, or if you look at notes or try to make connections with what has happened before, you're carrying on the dialogue alone. That's a monologue – a conversation with yourself about their stuff. When you do that, you have lost connection and any question you ask when they come out of their silence will be based on where you think they

---

16 Kline (2020)
17 Ibid

were when they went in and where you think they might be now. In fact, you have no idea where they are or what to do next. Unless you ask them.

When they emerge, check in. That might sound something like:

- Where are we now?
- What are your insights so far?
- What's your question now?

Notice that these are all future focused. Asking what happened is a request for them to recount the process they have just been through in the silence. You don't need to know that, unless they choose to tell you.

Your perceptions of silence will be different from the people with whom you are in conversation. Claire mentioned an incident in *Simplifying Coaching* where she had harsh feedback from a delegate: 'That silence was two minutes long. It was brutal. You should have said something.'[18] Before she had a chance to respond, the thinker said: 'What silence?' The thinker was busy doing good work, so the silence felt natural to her. The art was for Claire to notice how long it needed to last and be ready when the thinker came back. If you are not comfortable with long silences, it may be a sign that you have work to do.

3. They are stuck or do not have an answer – they are uncomfortable and hoping you will say something and make it less awkward

Awkward silence could be described as *frozen* or *get-me-out-of-here* silence. The thinker isn't thinking. They squirm inside, stare at you, or away from you, with a silent 'please say something' in the hope that you will break the silence. It is deeply uncomfortable. Ty Tashiro, author of *The Science of Why We're Socially Awkward and Why That's Awesome*, describes awkwardness as 'a deviation from

---

[18] Pedrick (2020)

a minor social expectation' where 'your mind is telling you – you should be alarmed and you should try and correct your behaviour.'[19] No wonder it feels so difficult - they have been triggered.

Mishandling frozen silence can erode trust. It can happen when the thinker was referred for coaching and isn't quite sure what it's for. They might be expecting you to be the expert, might not want to do the work, or may be new to a conversation where there is an expectation that they will do some work themselves. Some of the things they might be thinking are:

- What's the answer the coach wants me to give?
- I'm not being very helpful here!
- What made my boss suggest I have coaching?
- Please say something!

It is interesting how similar these are to the coach's self-doubt in silence!

When frozen silence is due to low trust, the thinker limits how much they want to tell you. This might be cultural or you might be touching sensitive topics where they do not want to go. It becomes difficult to go deep and get to the heart of the matter. The thinker becomes silent and distracted as they work out how to avoid sharing more.

Lucia worked with a woman who, for cultural reasons, was not used to sharing much about herself. Lucia felt a barrier between them when the conversation got closer to something she did not want to explore. Frozen silence. Lucia asked: 'I am sensing a barrier when we talk about this and yet I feel that you put emphasis on it. Is it something you want to handle on your own?' She nodded. They implicitly agreed that it is OK to not share everything and Lucia did not need to know what she did not want to share. Making this explicit made it safer for her to continue with her train of thought, knowing that her boundaries would be respected.

---

[19] Tashiro, TED Talks.

Sometimes silence will be frozen and it will be uncomfortable for you both. If you are going to minimize it, and learn to manage it well, you will need to get over your own discomfort with silence. And if you love silence and overuse it, you also need to find a way of working together that serves the thinker.

TRY THIS

- Be clear you are here to do some work and for them to think. Instead of saying *What would you like to talk about?* or *What is the problem?*, ask questions that suggest that this is work! When someone comes with lots of stuff, invite them to download for a contained amount of time, and then ask *What's the work we need to do together today?*
- When you notice that someone doesn't want to disclose and that they are freezing, name the thing and invite them to continue to do the work. Agree not to ask what it is.

---

4. I-don't-want-to-be-here silence

Claire was coaching on a management development programme and recalls one delegate in particular:

> Everyone was offered a single coaching session. This particular delegate had spoken up several times criticizing others. She arrived in the room for her coaching and sat down. I told her that she didn't need to stay if she didn't want to be there. She stayed in her seat and looked at me.

Every single person we coach is our teacher, especially the ones where we feel annoyed or afraid. This is where we do our best learning as we co-create something when we have no idea what to do. Unless we name what's happening, we will be taking responsibility for making the coaching work. And we will be doing too much.

> Claire said something like *Can I say what I see? I am noticing some strong feelings and it feels like there's some deeper stuff going on?* The delegate nodded. Inside Claire was thinking *What on earth do I do now?* This is where courage and not knowing count. *I wonder whether you don't want to talk about it?* Nod. They spent an hour in conversation. They never named the thing. Only that person will ever know what changed. But she looked completely different.

5. The coach is unsure about the next question to ask

When you believe that your questions are the most important thing you do, and you are unsure what to do, you'll go quiet while you come up with a question. As soon as you make the I-am-about-to-speak-wait-a-minute sound or gesture they will stop thinking and respectfully wait for you. This is panic, not inner silence, for the coach. We are working it out and making our own sense out of what we saw, heard or sensed.

6. The coach's silence feels imposed

When you love silence more than is useful for the thinker, you can slow down their processing by taking control of the pace. This can feel like enforced silence. The thinker will stop thinking and wait for you. It's like a magnet drawing the thinker into your preferences. It can be very annoying and can break trust. Someone in a supervision group described this as feeling like the coach was absent. When Claire walked the Camino in Spain (there's more on this in Chapter 2), within the first hour she had committed not to coach. Over five weeks, she had many conversations about deep stuff knowing that she couldn't be in dialogue with people if she never brought herself and her own story. Of course, provocative and useful questions were exchanged. But the people she met on The Way had not signed up to be coached. Claire recognized again that while coaching with consent can be experienced as a deep presence, without consent it can feel like absence and intrusion.

Nancy Kline has simplified and deepened work around listening in an extraordinary way through *Time to Think*.[20] And when someone has finished their work and is asked for the fifth time *What else do you think or feel or want to say?*, followed by a silence, people who described it as unhelpful will say that they had finished, but the facilitator looked like they knew better.

LOOK FOR THIS

- Try to recall the different kinds of silence that were present in your last coaching session.
- Consider what might impact the length of your silence.
- Think about how the silence is impacting the thinker.

STAY IN CONNECTION

Everyone is different. When one of you has a different preference for silence from the other, you aren't in sync. In a recording, you will notice it in facial expressions. If you're looking away and they are looking at you, you are probably working out what to do next. You are also missing the facial clues that tell you whether they are thinking or waiting for you.

During the COVID-19 pandemic, coaches learned to have conversations online. You may love them or hate them. Working online is the best lesson in using silence to keep someone company while they think. Eye-to-eye contact is not uncomfortable because of the position of the cameras. When they take a question or observation

---

[20] Kline (2002).

and make it their own, they will look away a little so that they can do some good work. Online, you can keep full eye contact all the time, which makes it easy to see the movement – and to watch their eyes. Now it's easier to wait. They will look at you when they are ready to come back. Just don't look away! If you take notes or consult notes you have made before, you will lose connection.

GETTING READY TO DO SOME WORK

Coaching is very different from other dyadic conversations. Your job is to facilitate the other person's (or people's) thinking. Ask *What's the work we need to do together today?* so it is clear right from the beginning why you are here. Until you do that you can get stuck as they explain stuff to you or feel they ought to give you information so that you understand. Once they start working, they start thinking. And then silence happens.

TRY THIS WITH A PEER COACH

- When you are coaching, commit with your peer coach that you won't break the silence.
- Wait a second before you speak – then wait another second.
- Ask for feedback about the kind of silence they experienced.

SIGNS THAT SILENCE ISN'T THERE

When silence isn't being used well, you will notice very few pauses between what you say and when the thinker replies. The purpose of questions in coaching is to provoke thinking. It takes time to think.

Silence is being under-used when the thinker's thinking is interrupted too much by sounds from the coach – especially when your *I-hear-you* sound or movement feels more like *tell me all about it*! These minimal encouragers can facilitate silence or accidentally block it. When you get to the end of listening to a recording and you feel you are panting, it needed more space and more silence. There's more about movement and sound in Part II (see Chapters 8 and 10).

QUESTIONS TO THINK ABOUT

- What one thing have you learned about silence that you are going to try?
- What do you need to do to arrive still to a session?
- What needs to change for you to feel even more comfortable with silence?

When you are both using silence well, they will start thinking and do more work than if you were simply asking one question after another. When you are silent inside as well as on the outside, you can pay attention to what is happening to the human in front of you. It feels like waiting in the room while they have a conversation with themselves. Their silence is precious and it is what they need. When the silence is theirs, it can only support them to move forward. They will break it when they have done what they need to do. Welcome them gently when they come back. This keeps the conversation in flow.

Watch them. All the time.

CHAPTER 2
CONTROL AND NOT KNOWING

For her sabbatical, Claire walked the Camino de Santiago de Compostela with friends. Here she gives a personal example of the outcomes of her own 'not knowing':

We began training a year before we started our walk, reading endless books and websites. If we could walk 15 miles for two days in a row on hills and rough terrain, said the books, we would be ready enough. We minimized what we would carry in our rucksacks and set off. One of us spoke Spanish. One of us was a nurse. We had controlled what we could control. The rest was unknown.

On day 10, I had an agonizing pain in my foot. This wasn't in the plan. I hobbled about five kilometres to the next café. This was new territory. The bar owner got me a taxi and my companions walked on. I'd work it out! I didn't speak Spanish. It hadn't been the artfully packed rucksack or the training that had been doing the walking. It was my body. Now it was broken. I had to embrace not knowing, accept that I was not in control and find a different way. Or go home.

I bussed. My friends walked. In some places there was one bus a day and the timetables you could find didn't agree on where the bus left from nor what time it went! I had to trust that I would find a way forward with the resources I had and the people I would surely meet on the way.

WHY NOT KNOWING MATTERS

Coaching is not a play with a script that can be codified. It is improvisation. If coaching is a partnership, we can't be in control because we don't know what's going to happen. We often have no idea what to do and will need to work it out together along the way. It's not our training or the resources we carry in our metaphorical rucksacks that enable us to not know in coaching. Artful coaching means that we know that those things are there – but that it's our body, mind, spirit and energy that will be engaging in this conversation with the body, mind, spirit and energy of the thinker. Deepening our coaching requires us to get comfortable not knowing what to do next and letting go of the need to be in control. That needs courage. More of that in Chapter 6.

Coaching is unique. Your role is to facilitate someone else to do good work. When success in your education, work and life has come from knowing the right answer to a question or being the best at problem solving, it's a shock to discover that artful coaching is all about being OK with not knowing. The credibility, knowledge and confidence you have relied on before are about knowing what to do next and being seen to know. In that world, your natural response to not knowing might have been to learn a little more. To consult the internet. To read a book. To sign up to a master's or doctoral programme. These are about what to do, what to ask, what tools to use, what to explore, what the research says. These can be useful. They are great training for the journey ahead and give you useful resources in your coaching rucksack. Claire's body had to do the walking in Spain, not her training. Similarly, the human coach does the coaching. She could have trained and tweaked her rucksack for another year. A coach could take another training course. In the end, the only way to walk the Camino was to trust the preparation and take the first step. The only way to coach is to trust what is inside you – and do it!

The ICF talks about a coach's need to be 'comfortable in a space of not knowing'.[1] Artful coaching requires us to become so comfortable in knowing that we don't know what to do, that we are mostly doing it without artfully concealing our panic – because our panic is no longer there. The only way to learn that is over time and with practice.

The things that have got you this far in other careers are not necessarily what will enable you to be more deeply human in the room. Unlearning takes time. Coach Liz Price hosts *Unlearning Circles* and describes mastery as 'constantly hovering in the space between conscious and unconscious competence. Don't ever be too competent,' she says, 'when it comes to difference.'[2] Liz works with people who are racialized as white, have already begun personal work on anti-racism and want to dive deeper into their own biases. It's a useful and challenging way of looking at your own attitude to control and not knowing. Don't ever be too competent when it comes to coaching. Some unknowing is fundamental to your capacity to be present and work in partnership. You can't be, and will never be, fully in control.

THINK ABOUT

- What is your relationship with control?
- What would letting go feel like for you?
- What do you have to do to let go?
- What do you need to believe to be able to let go?

---

[1] ICF, *Updated ICF Core Competencies.*
[2] Price in conversation with Claire Pedrick, The Coaching Inn Podcast (March 2022).

WHAT NOT KNOWING LOOKS LIKE

Leadership coach Hetty Einzig describes one role of the coach as being 'the Fool'.[3] In literature and in history, Fools are different from other people. The Fool asks the innocent, not-knowing questions – not in service of being clever but to open up the conversation. 'How often does the coach set aside technique and theory and risk playing the fool?' she asks. Playing the Fool means stepping into a place in the conversation or the relationship where you have no idea what will happen. 'Being present in our not-knowing-what-to-do, without fear of looking stupid, trusting our presence alone and reaching out from that place of the still pool' is challenging.[4] It is exposing. It will feel out of control and risky. And it's where the deep work happens. 'As coaches, are we willing to sacrifice the gleam of professional status to ask the dumb questions, the really dumb ones?'[5] Being human requires not knowing, humility and courage.

We are often asked what technique we would use in a specific scenario. Many coaches learn step-by-step models that should guide them to success. We believe that this need for structure comes from the desire to control, to fit within a model. Even following the arc – the beginning, the middle and the end of a conversation – having a list of powerful questions and learning even more tools respond to a need to add order to something we cannot control completely.

How do you gather enough inner confidence to risk letting go of control and going together into new and unknown territory, without a plan of what you will do when you get there? As you go into each conversation, everything you have been taught, learned and experienced prepares you for that moment. And nothing you have learned is of any use, unless it is useful for the thinker at that moment. What matters is how present you are. Artfulness is about holding your nerve.

---

[3] Einzig (2017)

[4] Ibid

[5] Ibid

Letting go of control is a challenge for growing coaches. The world of work gets us to constantly prove we are great at what we do, so we can be trusted and valued. Becoming more comfortable with not knowing is about who and how you are. There will be a moment in every coaching conversation where your need for control risks merging with your desire to be seen. That's the moment where you have to make a choice. Do you begin to work harder than they do, or can you continue to trust the process and the thinker more than you trust yourself?

We walk into the unknown. This can be terrifying, especially when you suddenly remember how much you are being paid, or you think about your obligation to the customer. How do you show you can deliver value? Sometimes you won't see it because much of their progress might happen between sessions. Coach and supervisor Alain Cardon talks about this moment 'of confusion [which] must be accepted, noticed, respected and overcome. The coach must search for trust within himself, in his client, in the situation, in the universe.'[6] When you can embrace that you are only human, you are able to let go of your need to control and find healthy ways to hold your anxiety and work out between you what you are going to do here and now.

'The goal of coaching isn't to make someone feel good. The goal is to break through a person's guise of knowing,' says coach Marcia Reynolds.[7] You can only do that by learning to hold this not-knowing space. The capacity to be present is far more useful than artful questions, tools or techniques. Embodying by simply being present is a lifelong learning journey. 'From birth to death we are engaged in an ongoing process of control,' observes Psychologist Dr Tim Carey. 'People let go of control by producing a particular feeling or experience. Reliably producing a particular feeling by using different behaviours and thoughts is the process of control. So people let go of control by controlling!'[8]

---

[6] Cardon (2011)

[7] Reynolds (2020b)

[8] Carey (2016)

LOOK FOR THIS

Reflect on the last coaching session you had by asking yourself these questions:

- How much of a plan did I have before I went in (or by the time the thinker finished the story)?
- How many times did I look for a tool?
- How did these things impact the direction of the conversation?
- What would I need to change to believe that the thinker might have the best questions for me to ask?

WHAT NOT KNOWING FEELS LIKE

Not knowing can feel challenging and uncomfortable at times. You may feel exhilarated (*bring it on!*) or terrified (*get me out of here!*). Not being in control does not mean that your work is chaotic, dangerous or out of control. At the beginning of the conversation, if you rightsized the work, you agreed on some boundaries. You agreed what you were going to do, how you were going to do it and how you would know you have done it. Or you agreed that you didn't know any of those things, knowing that you could work them out when it became a bit clearer. Not being in control happens – pretty much in every conversation – when it turns out that what you agreed is not actually the work at all. The stuff, the emotion or the systemic context feel enormous and overwhelming. The edge of what feels out of control for you will feel different for the thinker. The art is to hold the boundaries and not to take over.

When the work you are doing no longer feels safe enough for one or both of you, the conversation is on the way to being out of control. You need to work out together what to do well before this. Never being out of control requires the thinker to feel safe enough to do deep work with you. Unless you make it a normal practice to check in regularly with the thinker, you will never know whether what you are experiencing as fine, in fact, feels out of control for them. You may have crossed a boundary. It is not always possible to re-establish enough trust to continue to do deep work.

Control and not knowing are interconnected. If the thinker thinks or feels that you are in control, they will be following you. 'In coaching,' says Marcia Reynolds, 'the person must trust that the intention of the interaction is their development, not to say what's expected.'[9] That tolerance of not knowing and capacity to not be in control means that 'the need to protect and defend oneself is regulated down in both client and coach, creating optimal conditions for exploration and change.'[10]

You both need to be safe enough to tolerate feeling uncomfortable and have the courage to do the work. It is not your role to decide whether this is safe enough. Ask them. And then see, hear and sense their answer. Are they pleasing you and saying what's expected? Or are they saying what they mean? More of this in Chapter 4.

SIGNS THAT WE ARE TOO MUCH IN CONTROL

Over-planning, so that we look competent, undermines our capacity for not knowing. Coach and supervisor Beatrice Zornek describes what an external demonstration of competence looks like:

> You only need one client who answers every other question with 'I don't know' to see the principle of 'efforting' at play. You'll find yourself at the end of a session, having exhausted all your brilliant questions, asking yourself what else you can ask them in the next 11 sessions they've already paid for. But if you really think of it, 'efforting' has the resonance of a rescuer mindset. And that's the dark side of coaching.[11]

---

9 Reynolds (2020b)

10 Ibid

11 Zornek in conversation with 3D Coaching (2022).

An awful lot of coaching happens where the coach doesn't let go of control. The coach is leading. People answer the questions we ask them. When we lead, they follow: *Clearly my coach knows more about how to work through this than I do – let me do what they suggest.* The risk now is that they stop thinking.

QUESTIONS TO THINK ABOUT

- How do you empower the people you coach?
- What do you see in them that makes you know they are feeling empowered?
- Where have you taken more control than necessary?
- What needs to happen for you to let go of control?

FEARS THAT LEAD TO CONTROL

Hetty Einzig references a survey of the top five fears of CEOs.[12] Appearing foolish is at the top. The other four are underachieving, impostor syndrome, appearing vulnerable and being verbally attacked by colleagues. Do those same fears impact us and our ability or willingness to let go of control? Some of the descriptions we hear coaches use about themselves include:

1. Control freak
2. Perfectionist
3. Overthinker
4. Impostor syndrome

Let's look at how these relate to control and not knowing.

1. Control freak

On her Camino walk, Claire's rucksack had to be seven kilograms. She had no space for anything that was not essential. That's like

---

12 Einzig (2017)

coaching. The rucksack you take into a session will contain some of the tools and techniques you have learned that make you feel in control. It's safe and you can use them if you need to. You may not need any of them. Can you begin each conversation with empty hands and no intention to pick up a tool unless you agree together it could be useful? Can you take only what is inside you – and trust that what you will co-create together will be enough? 'Don't take what's in your head either,' said team coach Georgina Woudstra, in conversation with Claire. Team coaching requires an even greater capacity to not know.

When you exercise too much control, the conversation loses flow and starts following your plan rather than the thinker's exploration. You want to be seen to do a good job. A not-knowing mindset means that you won't have a plan B for running the session when you discover you don't know what to do. Plan B might manage your need to be in control. Putting it down requires courage and vulnerability. And is part of the work to consistently work in partnership with ease.

Lucia witnessed this when she was watching a recording with Alex.[13] Alex described the thinker as not being in a productive place. Alex was freaking out because he could not help her move forward from a low energy state. Alex chose a plan B to regain control and feel more comfortable that she could make progress. But what did the thinker need or want? Maybe she needed to grieve and sit with her emotions. Maybe it was not time for her to move on. The only way Alex would have known what to do was to ask her.

Remember that a successful outcome of every session is that the thinker has moved forward a bit. It is not that you have covered everything on their list or that they feel like you would like them to feel. Success does not come from your extensive reading of books or a script on what you should be saying in this conversation. You don't know. You can't control it. You're going to have to work this one out together.

---

[13] Name changed to protect privacy.

'Humans are not brilliant at not knowing. We like to think we know everything,' says Nancy Kline.[14] Some of us like to control everything. No coach can fully tolerate not knowing in every single coaching conversation. Sometimes you will simply be unable to hold your not-knowing nerve. Both the coach and the thinker need to hold not knowing together. When the thinker is anxious about their not knowing, and asking you for certainty, the power of projection can be a tough one to notice, let alone manage, and it increases the pressure on you even more.

For the first time in history, everyone in the world had a common experience of not knowing during the COVID-19 pandemic. We learned that we cannot control everything. 'There was no room for superheroes,' observed Professor Veronica Hope Hailey.[15] There is no room for superheroes in coaching either. When we intentionally or accidentally fill that role, we are taking over. Until we can tolerate the discomfort of not being in control, it will be hard to work with someone who is feeling out of control. Out of control happens when we are both panicking and fear has taken over. The art is to inhabit the spacious place where we are neither in control nor out of control.

2. Perfectionist

This book is not an instruction manual about how to be perfect. You are responsible for holding the work together, in partnership. It is not all down to you. It does not need to be perfect. You will make mistakes. There will be moments when you have absolutely no idea what to do next. Claire listened to a recording when a very experienced coach got lost. They managed to turn the conversation round by asking quite an average question that made the thinker think. You can recover. It's never too late as long as you don't make a thing about it because if you do, that brings the focus back to you and not the thinker.

---

14 Kline (2020)
15 Hope Hailey (2021)

We can never fully master this art. Every single conversation is a blank canvas that you will co-create together – even when you have worked with someone many times before. It's easy to think: *I've got this. I know how to coach a person like this.* You don't. Musician Moby says, 'Whenever I've had success, I never learn from it. Success usually breeds a degree of hubris. When you fail, that's when you learn.'[16] Self-confidence is important. You need to know you can do this well. Hubris is too much self-confidence. Perfectionism brings an assumption that you won't make mistakes. You will. Everyone we have coached when it feels like something went wrong has been a teacher to us – as long as we are willing to learn. We don't know how to work with anyone unless we ask them.

As much as it is useful to evaluate concerns and frustrations about what went right or wrong through reflective practice, you also need to be comfortable with not knowing how a conversation will go.[17] When you work hard to be good, you may lead more than is useful. Good enough is great. All coaches make mistakes. In every conversation there are just one or two questions that unlock the conversation. You can't plan, predict, rehearse or control them. And they are never the questions that you have in your pocket.

Watching recordings of your coaching can give useful feedback on whether you were trying to win. Supervision is another place to dig deeper into what happens inside you when it feels like things are going wrong. Sometimes your own stuff might get in the way of relaxing into the flow of the process. It can make you become too big and take control. That's not humility. That may usefully be explored in deeper work, for example, with a therapist.

3. Overthinker

Organizational psychologist Professor Adam Grant advocates the power of knowing that you don't know. His book *Think Again* is a

---

[16] Moby (2009)

[17] Reflective practice happens when you take time after a session to consider what was happening and what you are learning. There is more on this in Chapter 12.

treatise on keeping an open mind.[18] It is easy to overthink a question and do a quick analysis of what you are hearing in order to get a sense of what the problem is so that you can plan what you might do next in this or future sessions.

When we overthink, or when we think we know, we aren't doing our job. 'Scientific thinking [rethinking] favours humility over pride, doubt over certainty, curiosity over closure. When we shift out of scientist mode, the rethinking cycle breaks down, giving way to an overconfidence cycle.'[19] Artful coaching is about holding the space for someone else to explore. To facilitate their curiosity requires an ability to not overthink even if we then have to manage emotional overwhelm in the room. Ours or theirs.

QUESTIONS TO THINK ABOUT

- What's your own experience and feelings about overwhelm?
- How sensitive are you?
- How much are you at risk of allowing your sensitivity to influence your coaching?

People have a strong gravitational pull to get out of not knowing and into control as quickly as possible. Not knowing is uncomfortable. In *The Advice Trap*, author Michael Bungay Stanier describes the three personas of an advice monster that we use to manage our anxiety:[20]

- You must have the answer! If you don't Tell-It, nothing will get solved and we'll fail.
- You must be responsible for it all! If you don't Save-It and rescue everyone and everything, we'll fail.
- You must stay in control! If you don't Control-It and manage it all, we'll fail.

---

[18] Grant (2021)

[19] Ibid

[20] Bungay Stanier (2020)

Put down the advice monster, listen to what is being said and stop overthinking the next thing you'll say. This is the heart of artful coaching.

4. Impostor syndrome

Impostor syndrome was first described in a 1970s paper from psychologists Pauline Rose Clance and Suzanne Imes about high-achieving women who were afraid of being found out to be a fraud.[21] It's now recognized that '70% of people will experience at least one episode of this impostor phenomenon in their lives.'[22] This is not always negative. Supervisor Fiona Adamson asked Claire, 'Would you like yourself if you didn't have impostor syndrome?'

Clinical psychologists Jaruwan Sakulku and James Alexander, have shared some insights into the impostor phenomenon which can be seen in coaching:[23]

- Over preparation
- The need to be the best
- Superhero with perfectionist goals
- Fear of failure
- Denial of competence and not accepting praise
- Fear and guilt about success

When confidence is a problem, a coach might feel the need to learn more. However much training you have done, it is never enough because the story you tell yourself is *I'm not good enough*. The best measure of the impact of coaching might come months or years after the work has ended. No wonder that it's tempting to prepare some tools and techniques to use now so that you can get instant feedback.

---

[21] Clance & Imes (1978)

[22] Gravois (2007)

[23] Sakulku & Alexander (2011)

Lucia was asked for a list of training courses that would make someone a great coach. She replied: *There is no such list because it's not about what we know, it's about who we are in the room.* It is not necessary to be a learning junkie to be an artful coach. In the coaching profession, there can be a perceived need to do coaching better. To do it right. More knowledge and tools might make you a better coach. So will a deeper dive into some of the qualities we outline here. You can coach at your best by simply being there for the thinker. What they need most of all is to be seen and heard.

QUESTIONS TO THINK ABOUT

In your last coaching session:
- What do you remember?
- What happened?
- What did you do?
- Where did you get lost?

EMBRACING NOT KNOWING IN LIFE

Like Claire, Lucia has experienced not knowing in her life, and embraced it, as she explains:

> When my family moved away from Italy in 2014, my husband Marco said, 'Do you realize we will always be foreigners from now on?' I did not fully understand what he meant until later. A couple of years on, we knew our home in a new country was temporary and often found ourselves talking about when to leave, wondering about our next destination without knowing where that would be. We enjoyed being exposed to multiple cultures but felt some discomfort not knowing where life would take us nor where we belonged. We are back in Italy for now, and still embrace it because we value our freedom more than

settling somewhere permanently. Being OK not feeling in control is something we had to learn in order to embrace the life we wanted to live.

In reality, you can't control everything. It is a choice whether to accept this. Not knowing is a muscle you can develop in life that will impact your coaching. 'You only are free when you realize you belong no place – you belong every place – no place at all. The price is high. The reward is great,' said poet and activist Maya Angelou in an interview for the Bill Moyers Journal.[24]

As coaches, we belong in every coaching relationship, and yet we don't belong in the thinker's life. Belonging is a theme for Lucia's family and is true for many people we work with who are in some kind of transition. Lucia developed her not knowing even further through a complete life change. We can't all move to other countries, and the coaching room is not the place to learn this. So, how can you develop your not-knowing muscle?

DEVELOPING THE NOT-KNOWING MUSCLE

Improv is 'a form of live theatre in which the plot, characters and dialogue of a game, scene or story are made up in the moment'.[25] The not-knowing presence developed in improv is similar to coaching presence. This is one way to learn how to respond to someone else when you don't know what you're going to say next. If you can get to do a live in-person improv class, do it. And if you feel uncomfortable reading this, definitely do it!

Improviser Pippa Evans shares some exercises that you can do on your own to develop your not-being-in-control muscles. 'To embrace life [or coaching], we have to give up control. We cannot have deep, nuanced relationships with people if we have decided exactly how we want them to be, rather than responding to how they

---

[24] Angelou, 'Race, Morality and Lessons to a Daughter'.
[25] The Hideout Theatre.

are.'[26] This might mean dropping a question or a train of thought when it's no longer relevant and the thinker has moved on. It's about choosing not to speak when the thinker is busy thinking. It's about flexibility and resilience. 'Complete control,' says Pippa, 'stops any ability to adapt and be creative in the moment.'[27] That's why what you co-create is almost always more valuable than any tools or techniques you might have up your sleeve. You don't need to show you are bringing value to the process. More of you is not necessarily better.

Here are some examples of being-OK-not-being-in-control in coaching. You ask the thinker:

- *What do you want to do with this overwhelm?* (staying with feelings) instead of asking *What makes you less overwhelmed?* (moving to action).
- *And now?* because you have no idea about what to do next – and that is OK.
- *What question should I ask you now?* when you feel they are getting to an answer because you recognize they know better.

TRY THIS WITH A PEER COACH

Practice coaching together and choose to do one of the following:
- Every time there is a choice, let the thinker choose the direction.
- Only ask questions with less than five words.
- Assume you know what they are talking about as you begin – so no questions about the story.

---

[26] Evans (2021)

[27] Ibid

As you get more familiar with not knowing, and sharing control, partnership becomes easier. Your role is to facilitate, and you share responsibility for what happens. When things go well, you share the joys, and when the conversation becomes more difficult, you share responsibility for finding your way. Now you can spend more time offering what you notice and less time planning what to do next. This makes the work more effective for the thinker – because it is in their work that change happens.

CHAPTER 3
HUMILITY

Have you ever heard a coach say: *How can I be more humble?* We seek to be better at our craft – more knowledgeable, more artful, more present, more known for doing a great job. More expert, maybe? We want to be confident that we know what we are doing.

'There are some aspects of life,' says coach Chris Holmes, 'where you can really shine and be appreciated by the world for your stellar wisdom and expertise. Let me be clear: coaching is not that place. The first ingredient in the chosen mindset of coaching is humility.'[1] And when people have chosen to work with you, charisma may be the thing that got them in the room. German sociologist Max Weber described this as 'a certain quality of an individual personality, by virtue of which he is set apart from ordinary men and treated as endowed with supernatural, superhuman or at least specifically exceptional powers or qualities.'[2] There is work to be done.

WHAT IS HUMILITY?

The word humility comes from the Latin *humilis* (low) or *humus* (ground or grounded). While modesty is hiding our abilities and achievements, humility is being aware that we are people with our own good and bad characteristics. It impacts how people experience us when we interact with them and how we connect emotionally to build positive relationships based on trust. Humility requires honesty and vulnerability.

---

[1] Holmes (2020)

[2] Weber (1958)

This is not false modesty. It is great when you know that you are a good coach. And in every conversation, you need to manage your ego so that you can be useful and allow the thinker to generate new thinking. This takes courage because you are stepping into the unknown together. 'Here-and-now humility,' says business theorist and psychologist Edgar Schein, is the 'key to building positive relationships with those upon whom we are dependent because it reveals our genuine interest and curiosity in others as critical partners.'[3] Humility is what allows you to make each conversation all about them.

Leadership practitioners Edward Hess and Katherine Ludwig define humility as 'a mindset that results in not being self-centred, ego-defensive, self-enhancing, self-promotional and closed-minded.'[4] They explain how having an accurate view about our own limitations, and a low focus on ourselves, enables us to be open to new ideas and appreciate other people's contributions. Humble people focus their attention on others rather than on themselves, demonstrating qualities like curiosity, openness, authenticity, respect and a not-all-about-me attitude. Edward and Katherine describe key behaviours that demonstrate and enhance humility: quieting our ego, shutting down the voices inside our heads to lower our emotional defensiveness, being empathetic and open-minded, and focusing on the value and role of the thinker in a co-created process.

Humility is part of presence – being with another. It comes from an internal stance where you can give your full attention while at the same time being unattached to the outcome. Claire describes this as 'being attentively not bothered.'[5] If coaching is a partnership, you need to be equal enough. The coach is in the wings. It's the thinker who is on the stage.

---

[3] Schein (2013)

[4] Hess & Ludwig (2017)

[5] Pedrick (2020)

QUESTIONS TO THINK ABOUT

Think about your last few coaching conversations.
- Where can you recognize humility?
- What was challenging for you about demonstrating humility?
- When do you think more humility was needed?

WORKING WITH OUR OWN EMOTIONS

Lucia gives a personal example here of trying to open up the emotions of a family member:

One of my challenges as a mum has been helping my son, who used to lack awareness of his own emotions and struggled to communicate them in a constructive way. After an argument with his brother, I'd see him fill up with anger until he burst into tears. When I asked him what he was feeling, or what was making him angry, he could only say 'nothing'. It seemed too difficult for him to give a name to his emotions. Following the advice of a friend, an experienced child psychologist, I printed out a bunch of names of different emotions, with the intent to teach him a vocabulary that could help him interpret and navigate what he was feeling. It worked.

Brené Brown, who has done extensive research into shame, vulnerability and leadership, describes what Lucia observed: 'Language shows us that naming an experience does not give the experience more power; it gives us the power of understanding and meaning.'[6]

---

[6] Brown (2021)

In order to work with emotions that show up during a session, you need to be dealing with your own stuff enough so that you can manage yourself when others bring their stuff. This demonstrates *emotional intelligence*. It takes humility to notice:

- your own actions and behaviours;
- whether they are consistent with what you say;
- the impact they have on others;
- how you might project your emotions onto someone else.

How can you manage all this and remain a neutral observer and listener? Working this through in supervision, or reflective practice, is also an act of humility. 'Until we can receive with an open heart,' says Brené Brown, 'we're never really giving with an open heart. When we attach judgement to receiving help, we knowingly or unknowingly attach judgement to giving help.'[7]

Marc Brackett, founding Director of the Yale Center for Emotional Intelligence, helps people work through emotions using the acronym RULER (recognition, understanding, labelling, expressing and regulating).[8] Safety guidelines on a plane say put on your own oxygen mask first. Working through this process can be the emotional equivalent of putting on an oxygen mask. It is a great lesson in encouraging and not knowing if you are new to feeling your feelings. You may decide to do this in supervision or with a trusted someone.

- **Recognition**. Understand when new emotions pop up by noticing what is happening in your body, energy or thoughts: *What am I feeling?*
- **Understanding**. Identify what caused the emotion. You may not be ready to answer this or think there will be a better

---

[7] Brown (2020)
[8] Brackett (2019)

time to deal with it. 'We need to listen for the underlying cause that fuels the emotion,' says Brackett.[9]

- **Labelling**. Being able to name that emotion: *What is the one word that describes how I am feeling?* You cannot deal with emotions if you do not name them. If you need more insight around naming emotions, Brené Brown's *Atlas of the Heart* is an excellent resource.[10]
- **Expressing**. Communicate the emotion to others: *How can I (or can I) share how I am feeling in a useful way?*
- **Regulating**. Being able to choose your emotional reaction instead of being dominated by it. *What am I going to do about this feeling?* Regulating might start with taking a deep breath to get a bit of distance before you can decide how to deal with the emotion. 'Emotional regulation is not about NOT feeling', or controlling and suppressing what you feel, but rather 'giving ourselves and others permission to own our feelings – all of them,' says Brackett.[11]

HOW DO I MANAGE MYSELF?

Perspective matters. In order to listen to and be present for others, let's listen to our whole selves. Some of us prefer coaching from the head (mind), the body or the soul (spirit). Notice your somatic responses, emotions, reactions, thoughts – what you recall from your memories and more. It is easy to merge your own experiences with what you hear and make your own meaning. That meaning is then filtered through your own assumptions and beliefs, rather than coming from real observable data. We aren't being humble when we think we can logically work out their stuff rather than facilitating them to work it out for themselves.

---

[9] Ibid

[10] Brown (2021)

[11] Brackett (2019)

It is not just who they are, but also who we are in the room that might influence their energy and the flow of the conversation. Be curious about what is happening for them and listen wholly to what is being communicated, verbally and non-verbally, as well as to what is not being communicated at all. Our own emotions, thoughts and shifts in pace, tone or position impact the space between us and we have to be conscious and intentional about how we use them. Managing self means recognizing that it is not for us to encourage the thinker to move in a direction that has worked for us. Humility requires us to recognize that the story we are hearing is not our story.

Everyone will have a different development journey. If you know that emotions are getting in the way of your coaching, it may be useful to seek peer support, supervision or therapy.

'Great listeners... help people approach their own views with more humility, doubt and curiosity. When people have a chance to express themselves out loud, they often discover new thoughts,' says Adam Grant.[12] How you demonstrate your humility and listen enables the thinker to be more grounded in their thinking.

QUESTIONS TO THINK ABOUT

- What's your preference?
- Do you coach from your head, heart or soul?
- How difficult is it for you to understand and regulate your emotions?
- How do you use your body in coaching?

QUIETING OUR EGO

We have not seen humility in any list of coaching competencies. If coaching is a conversation between two people about one of us,

---

[12] Grant (2021)

that they (or someone else) are paying for, it takes humility to be willing to give the thinker the limelight in the conversation and to keep out of our own stories, ideas and advice. How can we give them space to think if the voice inside our head is saying we need to make a success of this and have value to add here?

We are wired to win. This comes from the two biggest fears of humans, which Brené Brown says are not being good enough and wanting to be worthy of love and belonging.[13] Former English cricketer Steven Sylvester describes how 'the pursuit of winning for one's self significantly increases our likelihood that we become selfish as we seek to protect, boost our self-esteem and avoid fear through winning.'[14] In *Detox Your Ego,* Steven interviewed top level sports people, finding that those who were most successful and became world champions managed to let go of being self-absorbed in their pursuit of winning. They then saw a deeper purpose in becoming world champions. They discovered a set of values, behaviours and beliefs that allowed them to go beyond the desire to win. They found out how to fully express themselves as they moved from a *selfish* to a *selfless* state by seeing how others – a community, team or family – could benefit from their success.

At the end of a coaching conversation, we have heard people say: *That was amazing, thanks for helping me to move forward!* It is easy to take the credit. Humility in coaching is about recognizing the qualities they demonstrated in the room and their courage to do the work.

'Self-acceptance,' says positive psychologist Courtney Ackerman, 'comes from our achievements.'[15] We feel proud when we perform well and put effort into demonstrating our abilities, so that we can prove we are worthy. There's nothing wrong with pride in our work. But we also need humility to keep things in perspective. In other successful careers, 'our competence has... built our credibility,' says

---

[13] Brown (2012)

[14] Sylvester (2016)

[15] Ackerman (2018)

author Stephen Covey.[16] When people attribute great results to us rather than to the work we have done together, we can become pedestalled. They elevate what we did or said and it's human nature to accept the feedback they give – even when the win is theirs. This is not about us winning. It is not our race to win.

TRY THIS WITH A PEER COACH

Watch back a recording with your peer coach, or practice coaching in a triad or quad and ask for feedback on these questions:

- How big or small are you?
- What does winning look like for you? The thinker? Both of you?
- Did you outshine the thinker? How?

SHARING RESPONSIBILITY

When we think we know best, there will always be an impact on partnership. Coach and academic Hélène Seiler describes her journey into partnership:

> Once I had fully internalized that my client was a learning partner, it allowed me to let go of the assumption that I was solely responsible for the success of the coaching process. Instead, I shifted to sharing responsibility with [them].[17]

We start to lead instead of asking where it might be useful to go. Then we lose confidence because we are unsure whether the thinker is getting value. 'Listening well,' says Adam Grant, 'is more than a matter of talking less. It's a set of skills in asking and responding. It

---

16 Covey (2006)
17 Seiler (2021)

starts with showing more interest in other people's interests rather than trying to judge their status or prove our own.'[18]

Growing coaches often come up with a hypothesis about the thinker's situation and ask questions to prove or disprove it. Lucia's colleague, Karen Bruns, calls this confirmation bias.[19] You might see the thinker about to have insight. Unless you let them see it first, you can easily pull or push them by telling them what the meaning is. Then you win. You have told them. The moment of insight has gone. Transformation comes when they realize things for themselves.

As coaching becomes more artful, the pull to get to meaning when you can see it reduces. How can you demonstrate the humility to co-create the place where the thinker is beginning to make meaning – and then step back and let them make it themselves? Imagine being in the middle of a difficult coaching conversation when you're afraid of getting stuck. Winning means getting out of the stuck-ness as quickly as possible so that you look as if you know what you are doing. You might draw on a tool or a stock question to get in flow. This puts a lot of responsibility on you as a coach and can make you feel useless and frustrated: *I should have asked this question* or *I should have done this instead* are phrases we hear from coaches. You are both stuck.

Winning is not about you and what you do in the room. This isn't your gig. You share responsibility here! There is a moment in almost every conversation where things get uncomfortable and you can choose to take the easy way out and ask a question. That changes the subject. It's more comfortable, feels safer and there is less risk. Changing the subject gets the conversation moving again. And now it's likely to be transactional. You won. At a price.

If your deeper purpose is to enable someone else to move forward, the focus becomes being fully present, noticing, helping them make their own meaning. Not needing to win means that you

---

[18] Grant (2021)

[19] All the references to bias in this chapter come from Karen Bruns's work. Available from: https://monarchcoachingllc.com

are no longer attached to an outcome. You trust that, even if they move things forward just a little during the session, there will be further movement in between sessions. They own the change they want for themselves. Your ambition changes from making sure you are seen to do a good job – winning – to empowering them to discover the insight. You focus on sharing responsibility for what happens in the space between you.

Letting the thinker win in the moment where you feel exposed can lead to deeper transformation. An artful coach sits with discomfort a second or two longer – with absolutely no idea what you are going to do next, and with no plan B question lined up. This is a risk. It might not work. It enables greater depth where new awareness and insights will emerge for the thinker. You can stay in sync and are there waiting for them every time they return from their thinking. When you stop taking responsibility for your own success, there is suddenly much more energy in the room. This takes work on not knowing, silence and an enormous amount of courage. It is a marvellous thing to witness someone discover that they know exactly what to do.

When you move from wanting to be seen to do the right thing to dancing with them, you have stopped controlling the conversation and are in fuller partnership. Not everyone who comes for coaching can tolerate this level of partnership. Sometimes they are not ready to do the work. They actually want you to win!

Friends and colleagues can keep us grounded. 'A [musical] conductor can be easily seduced by the public's extraordinary attention to his unique offering and come to believe that he is personally superior,' observes Ben Zander in *The Art of Possibility*.[20] After 20 years conducting orchestras, Zander realized that in the moment of doing the work, the conductor does not make a sound. He describes his journey from asking *How good am I?* to *How effective [am I] at enabling the musicians to play each phrase as beautifully as they [are] capable?* However qualified, knowledgeable or famous

---

[20] Stone Zander & Zander (2006)

we are, whatever adulation goes before us, we are only as good as the work we co-create in each session. Our job is to let someone else shine on the stage. Zander asks: 'How much greatness are we willing to grant people?'[21] How much work are we willing to allow the thinker to do?

WHAT ARE WE BEING PAID FOR?

When you are an employee, your coaching has no connection with what you are paid. Once you become a freelance coach, it's normal human behaviour to want to be seen to bring value for the money you charge.

Michael Bungay Stanier describes short-term gains which look fancy but are not sustainable. On the subject of knowing, he talks about the short-term 'prize: I'm always seen to be "adding value" with my ideas' and the shadow 'punishment: I believe my only way of adding value is by having an answer, a heavy obligation. I crowd out others' ideas.'[22] If you're doing pure coaching, you are not being paid to know. If you are hired to do hybrid coaching/mentoring, you may be being paid to know and if you try and add value quickly, you'll still be crowding out their ideas.

You are not paid for the number of words you use. You are paid to be present, to hold the not knowing and facilitate someone else to do some good sustainable work. In reality, many coaches feel that they are paid to be responsible for the progress the thinker makes.

Artful coaching is not about how great you are, nor how articulate. It's not about your worth or wisdom. It's about what happens in the other person as a result of your dialogue. Self-esteem is needed to coach when we will never know our full impact. Sometimes we don't get feedback because our work is hidden in confidential conversations. The results are theirs and may show up in weeks or months. By the time deep change is embedded in the thinker and

---

[21] Ibid
[22] Bungay Stanier (2020)

their wider system, it's unlikely that anyone else is interested in the fact that this was partly catalysed by a coach they have never met.

THINK ABOUT

- What is your attitude to value and money?
- How does humility impact what you charge?
- What needs attention?

FLATTERY

In the coaching relationship, navigating humility is like navigating power. When people give you flattering labels or power, it's easy to accept them even when it is your intention to stay humble. We are in an industry that pedestals people and creates gurus. We have experienced it ourselves. Every time we absorb adulation, we risk feeling just a little more special, superhuman even. That is about status. And status is about power. Who keeps you grounded?

Flattery is a gift offered with good intention. *I couldn't have done this without you* may be true. Whether the thinker has been promoted, nailed a presentation, found a better way to relate to another person or found the meaning of life, the transformation that is happening is their work and a result of what you did together. You did your part. And they did more! 'Humility does not mean thinking about yourself less but thinking less about yourself,' say Edward and Katherine.[23] Wise words for coaches.

When you are focusing on how good you are and what you are doing, you are thinking too much. You might become anxious about bringing value and get nervous if the thinker doesn't seem to be making progress. Then it is tempting to jump in and save them because you know best:

---

[23] Hess & Ludwig (2017)

- If I work hard enough, I'll get great results.
- They'll judge me on being an expert in this, so I have to show them what I know.
- I have to say this now because it's important.

All of these focus on winning. That's about you.

There is an important difference between self-confidence and humility. In coaching, self-confidence comes from knowing you have technical skills. Humility is about how important you think you are. Bringing them together influences how big or small you are in the conversation. When you are too big or small, it is difficult to co-create because you are not equal enough. You are not in partnership. How can you own the authority and the value that come from your technical skills without over-claiming?

When the thinker gives you power you don't deserve and you don't moderate, it becomes difficult to be humble. Do they come to you because you have a name that automatically assigns you power? Or because of the way you speak? When the partnership is working well, who takes the credit?

STATUS

In his article *The Psychology of Social Status*, Adam Waytz notes an observation made by neuroscientist Michael Gazzaniga:

When you get up in the morning, you do not think about triangles and squares and these similes that psychologists have been using for the past 100 years. You think about status. You think about where you are in relation to your peers.[24]

How good am I? and *How important am I?* are human questions.

Status is real and partnership requires us to be equal enough. In *Helping,* Edgar Schein observes that anyone coming to a helping

---

[24] Waytz (2009)

relationship is automatically one down.[25] This concept comes from a 1950s comedy book, *One-upmanship* by British writer Stephen Potter: 'How to make the other [person] feel that something has gone wrong, however slightly.'[26] When the thinker arrives thinking we have the solution, they arrive one down. We are one up. Only partnership can level the difference a bit.

When you are working with a high-status person, they might arrive one up. Your presence and authority need to match theirs. Over-humility from you will be received as a lack of personal power. You will have to look a little bigger with strong assertive thinkers than you will with someone who is lacking in confidence. Across a number of sessions, a coach with a big ego will have less impact because there will be over-presence. Both of you will need to show your human side in the relationship in order to do some good work together.

When we are concerned with our own status, we don't easily recognize what others are doing. Recognizing someone's contribution means saying *I understand your effort, I am thankful for what you did, you are an example for others*. There is too little of this in the workplace. Positive reinforcement impacts morale and is an essential quality for leaders as well as coaches. Recognizing people's contribution reinforces a culture of gratitude and appreciation and bestows status. This applies beyond the coaching space.

Imagine your qualities are being acknowledged. What does that spark in you? Lucia intentionally gives positive feedback to people who look sad as they do a repetitive service job – like cleaners or baristas. Energy, motivation, pride, joy and care are some of the words that come up when she does this. Saying *I see you* is a deeply human encounter.

How can we say *I see you* to the people we coach? Coach Fran Fisher talks about exploring someone's relationship with a

---

[25] Schein (2009)

[26] Potter (1952)

challenge.[27] This is not just about what they are struggling with, it can be about what they can leverage or what makes them special. Lucia asks herself, *What is great about who they are being here and now?* An artful coach is able to recognize and acknowledge the thinker and the qualities they demonstrate in the room. You can notice and celebrate what's happening:

- You are demonstrating a lot of strength as you take responsibility for this.
- It takes a lot of courage to change things like you're doing.
- I admire your focus and determination to manage this change.
- As I hear your story, I'm impressed by your ability to stand up for yourself.

They might not get this from anyone else. It is a gift you can offer.

QUESTIONS TO THINK ABOUT

Think about the last time you coached someone who you perceive to have high status, or high personal power.
- What did you do to level up the difference?
- What was challenging for you?
- What can you do intentionally to level up before you enter the coaching conversation and as you begin?

SELF-PROMOTION

We are human people in an industry where it can feel like we're selling ourselves. Many coaches look for associate work so that someone else does the selling. If this is your first encounter with self-employment, you might find promotion a challenge. You might feel uncomfortable

---

[27] Fisher in a group conversation with Lucia Baldelli.

looking at coaches on LinkedIn and other platforms bigging up their bios and self-promoting. In 2022, coach Martin Carter wrote:

> You don't get to name yourself an 'influencer', a 'thought-leader', a 'disruptor' or whatever other band-wagon jumping BS you choose to pick. If someone or an organization of note has identified you as such, if you appear in an established publications 'top' list, if you rule the freakin' world then fair enough. If not, then enough already. Unless your title has been bestowed on you by someone of note then can we get a bit of honesty in your headlines. You're a coach, you're a blogger, you're an author.[28]

If you need to be financially independent from coaching, you need to manage the business side of things at the same time as developing artful conversations. There is a delicate dance between humility and self-promotion. We receive *get-to-six-figure-salaries-in-three-months* messages every day, which invite coaches to high levels of self-promotion. From time to time, Claire invites guests such as Martin Carter or coach and marketing expert Sarah Short to *The Coaching Inn* podcast to talk about marketing with integrity in a way that is honest without being self-promoting.

QUESTIONS TO THINK ABOUT

- How can we demonstrate humility using words to describe ourselves that do not over-claim?
- What does promotion with humility look like for your business?

---

[28] Carter (2022)

CONNECTION AND CARE

The internal transformation that makes us better coaches enables us to be deeply connected to others. Coaches need outward facing-ness and connection. William Damon, Professor of Human Development at Stanford University, discovered this in his research into how young people find purpose by 'engaging in something that the person finds absorbing, challenging and compelling, especially when it makes a valued contribution to the world beyond the self.'[29] This goes back to winning. What does winning for others look like?

'Confident humility supercharges our ability to earn trust,' says academic Rachel Botsman.[30] To connect effectively, we can build relationships based on trust, showing 'positive regard for people as human beings by indicating our interest in them.'[31] This is the authentic caring that comes from humility. Showing we care hugely impacts trust. It goes hand in hand with our ability to create intimacy in any conversation. Too often, particularly at work, we have transactional conversations about getting stuff done and we know nothing about others as individuals; we become self-absorbed in our work and in ourselves.

When humility is low and our focus is primarily on ourselves, we do not pay attention to others and their perception is that we simply don't care. The founder of *Trusted Advisor*, Charles Green, calls this 'self-orientation.'[32] We are humble when we demonstrate that it is not all about us because we care about the other person. 'No one cares how much you know until they know how much you care,' said former US president Theodore Roosevelt.[33] When we are in dialogue, we have to balance being present with them at the same time as maintaining enough of our own sense of self to continue the conversation in a way that is useful and engaging for them.

---

[29] Damon (2009)

[30] Botsman (2021)

[31] Hess & Ludwig (2017)

[32] Green (2011)

[33] Commonly attributed.

Our need to be over-present can get in the way of connection. This can look like:

- talking too much;
- explaining or rephrasing questions;
- discarding options that the thinker comes up with;
- lacking empathy for the thinker's emotional state.

TRY THIS WITH A PEER COACH

Watch a recording together where you are coaching and invite feedback from your peer. How does your peer think you are demonstrating humility in your interventions? Ask them to comment on your:

- silence;
- not knowing;
- questions;
- rightsizing/contracting.

We are people first. Then coaches. Like the world champions interviewed by Steven Sylvester, when we see value in the human work we do that is greater than our role as a coach, we can let go of being self-absorbed in demonstrating a great session and focus on who is benefitting from the process. Reflecting on what coaching means to us and why we want to work with others can help us change our attitude to winning. We can let go of winning for ourselves.

Humility means a shift from trying to demonstrate we are good enough, to working in service of the thinker. The moment we can become comfortable not knowing how the conversation will go, we can detach from worrying about our performance and we can both trust the process. This makes us less bothered about the specific outcome of a conversation and more focused on the greater purpose of enabling change over time.

In coaching, humility means that we don't overestimate how important we are. Let's believe that this person will be able to come up with their own solutions. While we are thinking that we have all the best ideas, our partnership will be impacted. We need to manage ourselves.

CHAPTER 4
VULNERABILITY

Vulnerability is something we all experience but perhaps don't express. Here, Lucia shares a personal example of vulnerability (and the outcome) as she moved from one country to another:

When Marco and I lived in Rome, we were consultants with long commutes. We had just had our two boys and wanted to look for opportunities in another country to improve our quality of life. I received a tablet for my birthday and started to polish my rusty English by watching TV series on the way to work. A few months later, I was hired by a company in Gibraltar (an English-speaking territory). We sold our house in Italy and moved to the heart of Andalusia in Spain. We were very excited, full of enthusiasm and my husband took paternity leave, which would keep his job open should we decide to return.

On day one, I attended a meeting with an offsite team. People spoke very fast. I couldn't understand and I became increasingly nervous. By the end of the meeting I had stopped listening. In my head, I was watching a movie about the upheaval of the last few months. I would be fired because of my poor English. When the meeting ended, my boss asked me if I had any questions. I stared for a while and then said, 'I did not understand what you were talking about.' That was the moment when I fully experienced vulnerability. I had exposed myself and my young family to a risk, I was being bluntly honest with this Englishman, felt lost and had no clue how to wake up from the nightmare.

This is vulnerability. 'It's having the courage to show up and be seen when we have no control over the outcome,' says Brené Brown.[1] We are vulnerable every time we move out of what feels comfortable to us. 'Vulnerability is not weakness; it's our greatest measure of courage,' she adds.[2] For Lucia's family it was the start of a life of opportunity, joy and multicultural exposure. Her boss was an incredible support in her professional growth and they lived in Gibraltar for nearly a decade.

Brené Brown defines vulnerability as 'uncertainty, risk, and emotional exposure.'[3] We are vulnerable when we say, *I don't know, I made a mistake, Let's work out what we need to do now*. This is a normal experience when we feel we're not in control. And we will sometimes feel vulnerable when we embrace not knowing.

Coaching is a people profession and yet we might struggle with showing our humanity. We might run away from uncomfortable feelings or suppress the fear that we experience when we don't know how to support the person who is paying us. Instead of arriving as we are, we work hard to avoid the shame of feeling exposed or unprofessional. We might feel anxious about not knowing what to say or uncertain about what to do. We may have been brought up to believe, or have assumed, that vulnerability demonstrates weakness and incompetence. This can lead us to avoid it.

Emotional vulnerability requires us to feel our feelings and acknowledge our emotions, which might include grief, shame, fear and disappointment. 'Vulnerability,' says Brené Brown, is 'the birthplace of love, belonging, joy, courage, empathy, and creativity.'[4]

---

[1] Brown (2015b)

[2] Ibid

[3] Brown (2015a)

[4] Ibid

If we want to bring creativity and innovation into our work, let's embrace the fear of knowing that we will make mistakes.

WHY VULNERABILITY MATTERS

In *Simplifying Coaching*, Claire spoke about how coaching is not about someone who is sorted helping someone who is not sorted.[5] Vulnerability means recognizing who we really are with varying degrees of imperfection. If you expect that the thinker will be brave, you will need to be brave. If you hope that they will be vulnerable, you will also need to be vulnerable. Vulnerable is not leaky. Brené Brown observed that 'vulnerability is the last thing I want you to see in me, but the first thing I look for in you.'[6] This demonstration of humanity invites the thinker to join you in sharing the risk and that's what deepens connection. Your capacity to bring and hold your own vulnerability is as important as building trust and creating psychological safety in the relationship. There's unlikely to be vulnerability without enough mutual trust.

One of Claire's favourite songs from The Killers mysteriously begins 'are we human, or are we dancer?' The inspiration is said to come from journalist Hunter S. Thompson who wrote that 'America is raising a generation of dancers, afraid to take one step out of line.'[7] Are we human or are we coach? Is our industry raising a generation of coaches who are afraid to take one step out of line?

If you're going to deepen the work that you will co-create in coaching conversations, there's a point where you will need to address your own stuff. Using your technical skills and being fully human enhances the partnership. Learning to embrace your vulnerability is part of this work.

The food industry has shaped how people eat – even when it does not serve our health. Coach training is a global industry, which

---

[5] Pedrick (2020)
[6] Brown (2015a)
[7] The Killers (2018)

shapes how people begin to coach. But coaching isn't just about what we have been taught, it is partly skill and mostly human.

Author and street artist Robert Drake says, 'to be human is to be broken and broken is its own kind of beautiful.'[8] This means being OK with not knowing what to do next. It means accepting that some things you do will be a mistake and that you will recover. You do not have to have all the answers. You do not need to learn the encyclopaedia of perfect questions. You do not have to know what to do next. You will work it out together.

QUESTIONS TO THINK ABOUT

- What is your current relationship to mistakes?
- How much do you give yourself permission to be vulnerable?
- What will be the impact on your coaching if you embrace vulnerability even more?

WHAT VULNERABILITY FEELS LIKE

'Your entire working life you've been told to be professional,' says author Kim Scott, 'too often, that's code for leaving your humanity at home.'[9] We can become too distant from someone when we wear our professionalism on the outside like military armour. Armour is heavy. It slows us down and makes it hard to keep up when the thinker is moving quickly. The journey to artful coaching requires us to honour the professional part of ourselves while demonstrating that we, too, are human. And much of our learning will emerge as we navigate the ups and downs of our own lives, especially the difficult bits. Artful coaching grows as we expand our development from what we do to who we are so that we can be more accepting of our own discomfort.

---

[8] Commonly attributed to RM Drake.
[9] Scott (2019)

The more we become comfortable with our vulnerability, the more we can tolerate not knowing. How can we be natural in the extraordinary space we are sharing with another person where our primary task is to listen and facilitate their thinking? Our desire to look like we know what we are doing and that we are professional enough can get in the way. Becoming technically perfect in coaching is an unreachable fantasy.

Most conversations build up to a moment where transformation happens. You can't predict when that will be nor what will trigger it. The art is to keep the conversation in flow so that the thinker keeps thinking, feeling and processing. Lack of flow is always the reason why a transcript can look perfect when the recording of the same conversation demonstrates a lack of partnership and connection.

The pressure that you put on yourself when you are coaching can be immense. That is a vulnerability trigger. You can choose to embrace it when you are willing to co-create the work every time you meet. There is always going to be a risk that it might go horribly wrong. You will always be vulnerable and unprepared. When you bring your vulnerability, you are still enough. That will build your confidence and guide you on the path to artful coaching.

Your confidence impacts how big or small you appear in the conversation. A coach lacking confidence while coaching an executive who is not moving forward might be thinking something along these lines:

They are stuck and I am not helping... I'd like to ask her to stand and experience making that jump she is talking about to see where it takes us – but every time I ask her to move, I feel awkward. I can't ask a leader to stand alone in a room and jump. She will think I am mad!

Here is a confident coach in the same situation:

I don't know what could get her unstuck. I sense if she changes perspective, she might gain some new insights. She used the word jump several times, maybe it'll be useful to actually jump. I'll ask if she is OK to try it out. I'll stand and jump with her, so that it doesn't feel odd. I'm confident that something might unlock. We just need to move this forward a little. Then she'll work on the insights that emerge.

Both coaches are vulnerable. A different level of confidence shifts the attention from you to the thinker – their experience, their stuck-ness, which is not yours to fix. By giving yourself permission not to have all the answers, the confident coach does not take on the thinker's challenge as if it was their own. Confident vulnerability allows you to be creative as you remain curious about what the process will unfold, trusting that something will change. Confidence in the process enables you to be vulnerable because the success of this conversation is a partnership between you, the thinker and the coaching process.

CONFIDENCE

Confidence is 'the messy process of learning and unlearning, practising and failing, and surviving a few misses,' says Brené Brown.[10] You will fall over in coaching. Where on the scale from under-confident to over-confident is enough for you?

Building confidence starts by identifying and growing competence. You want to get to a point where *you* believe you are good enough as a coach. This requires lots of learning and technical practice: the basics of a great beginning, a middle and an end to a conversation and how to say what you see. Practising, listening back to recordings and noticing the impact of your questions and observations on the thinker all build confidence using peer coaching, working with a mentor coach, and learning tools and techniques. You need to know how to *do coaching right* before you can make it your own, trust yourself and trust the process. This brings what

---

[10] Brown (2018)

Brené Brown describes as 'grounded confidence'. Bringing in your humanity is what makes conversations come alive because once you believe you are competent enough, you can finally begin to let go of performance anxiety. If it's important for your competence to be externally validated, you will be exploring professional accreditation. Whatever credential you have, the work on your humanity will last a lifetime.

QUESTIONS TO THINK ABOUT

- How confident are you as a coach?
- What do you say to yourself when you don't know what to do next?
- How would you like to respond differently going forward?

PRESENCE

The ICF describes coaching presence as a 'sense of complete ease and naturalness in conversation' where the 'coach does not have to "work" to coach'.[11] You can't see presence. Academic and coach Tünde Erdös describes it as 'a purposeful dynamic interplay that emerges as measurable non-verbal energy from the interpersonal interactions between coach and client through the doorways of the mind, body and heart.'[12] This is about being fully conscious in the here-and-now experience and recognizing that the dynamics of this dialogue are not just down to you. They are co-created.

Presence works when you are an appropriate size in your timing, tone, pace, position and volume of words. If you want some practice, Pippa Evans's book *Improv your Life* has some useful exercises where you can practise presence solo and/or in a group.[13] When you

---

[11] ICF (2019)
[12] Erdös (2021b)
[13] Evans (2021)

are present, you are fully aware of yourself and the impact you have. You embrace vulnerability enough to feel comfortable with whatever emerges in the room, for example, strong emotions, outbursts, tears or lack of forward movement. You know how to adapt your style with flexibility and confidence. You are, in the words of coach and author Doug Silsbee, in 'a state of awareness in the moment, characterized by the felt experiences of timelessness, connectedness and a larger truth.'[14] You give your full attention, trust the process and believe that the outcome is down to both of you.

Being open to what emerges is a very vulnerable place to be. Along with letting go of control, enough vulnerability enables you to have a *non-anxious-enough* presence. Rabbi Edwin Friedman came up with the concept of non-anxious presence. He also talked directly about being human and how people can turn to data to avoid the anxiety that comes from vulnerability.

> Despite its anxiety-provoking effects, the proliferation of data [also] has an addictive quality. Leaders, healers, and parents 'imbibe' data as a way of dealing with their own chronic anxiety. The pursuit of data, in almost any field, has come to resemble a form of substance abuse, accompanied by all the usual problems of addiction: self-doubt, denial, temptation, relapse, and withdrawal. Leadership training programs thus wind up in the co-dependent position of enablers, with publishers often in the role of 'suppliers'. What does it take to get parents, healers, and managers, when they hear of the latest quick-fix fad that has just been published, to 'just say no'?[15]

---

[14] Silsbee (2008)

[15] Friedman (2007)

TRY THIS

- List what you normally do or take with you into a session to make you feel less vulnerable.
- As an experiment, try going without these things and see what happens.

HOW TO BE VULNERABLE

You can only be vulnerable in the room and in the coaching relationship when you are doing your own work. If part of the unspoken psychological contract is that the thinker brings their humanity, then you need to bring yours. You will accidentally bring unprocessed stuff into the coaching space like an aura. You are only a part of the coaching process. The outcome of the coaching is not all down to you. Appropriately vulnerable confidence will build your capacity to be 'attentively not bothered.'[16] Supervision is a great place to explore this.

HAVING COMPASSION FOR OURSELVES

Coach and author John Blakey describes kindness as one of the leadership habits underpinning trust.[17] Kindness enables you to be as compassionate to yourself as you are to the thinker. Every coach makes mistakes. We do, all the time. The art of making mistakes is to manage yourself when they happen so that the mistake neither interrupts the thinker's thinking nor interferes with your capacity to listen and be present. Author Kristin Neff offers an invitation: 'Instead of mercilessly judging and criticizing yourself for various inadequacies or shortcomings, self-compassion means you are kind and understanding when confronted with personal failings.'[18] Brené

---

16 Pedrick (2020)
17 Blakey (2016)
18 Neff (2011)

Brown is more direct: 'We can only love others as much as we love ourselves.'[19]

It can be easier to be compassionate to others than to yourself. 'Love your neighbour as yourself' is a challenge that has underpinned the Christian faith for 2000 years for good reason.[20] If you want the people you coach to love themselves, you will need to demonstrate that you love yourself. Enough and not too much! Love requires compassion, empathy and accepting yourself as you are. When you are judgemental about your mistakes, you might do the same to others. When you become overly critical of yourself in a conversation, it reduces your capacity to hold the space, be present and notice what is happening in the thinker. When you start listening to the voices inside you, you make what's happening in the conversation about you. And when you make it about you, the thinker will pick that up. They might think: *You didn't unstick me… you didn't help…* Now it is about you!

Compassion enables you to silence some of the voices in your head that stop you listening to the thinker. If you are a perfectionist, demonstrating vulnerability can be harder. Becoming judgemental about your own behaviours or actions makes you sensitive to more negative information because that is data which signals threat. If you are someone who stays with the negative and goes over thoughts in your mind, over time this can undermine your self-esteem and interfere with your ability to be present in a conversation. Hyper focus on what's gone wrong before can mean you are listening to the ghosts in your heads and not the person who is right in front of you.

Learn from mistakes. And then leave them. As well as developing a forgettery of what people bring to coaching, it's useful to have a forgettery about what you think you did wrong. Not everything you will say or do is useful. As long as the thinker is getting new insights, you are doing a great job.

---

[19] Brown (2020)

[20] Matthew 22:39, Holy Bible, New International Version (NIV).

Self-talk is normal. When it is loud, it can get in the way. On a good day you accept it, understand why it's there and let it go. On bad days it's easy to feel inadequate and insecure. Feeding self-talk makes it grow. If you wake up in the night talking to yourself about something that went wrong in a session, you can tell the voice that it doesn't belong in your bed.

A way out of self-criticism is to 'understand it, have compassion for it, and then replace it with a kinder response.'[21] We invite you to be kind to yourself. Only then can you make an active effort to soften the critical voice, making it easier to reframe a negative thought into something kinder and more positive.

Coaches need to be able to respond to what is happening in the room as well as they can, be aware of what is happening in the moment, accept it and let go if it is not useful. This

> conscious awareness of the here and now allows us not to get lost in our thoughts and feelings. It puts us instead in a position to look at our own experience taking an outsider's perspective to make a conscious choice of what to do with it. We cannot control our thoughts and emotions, but 'we can change the way we relate to them'.[22]

What you bring into the coaching session has a lot to do with how you see and value yourself as a human. Claire's supervisor Fiona Adamson says, *Who you are is how you coach*. Growing coaches often think they aren't good enough. More experienced coaches learn to accept that their conversations will never be flawless and use self-awareness as a place to learn. Their critical voice is much quieter in the room, which gives them more headspace to pay attention to what they see, hear and sense is emerging.

---

21 Neff (2011)

22 Ibid

QUESTIONS TO THINK ABOUT

Think of a time when you remember your critical voice being loud in a coaching session. Ideally, watch a recording of a session when you know it happened.
- How did you respond to your self-talk?
- What impact did that have on you?
- What was the impact on the thinker?

SOME EXAMPLES OF HOW YOU MIGHT DEMONSTRATE VULNERABILITY

You are vulnerable when:

- **You say, *What do we need to do now?***
  Often it's unclear where you need to go next. If you like to line up questions in advance, you will follow your plan and take the lead. What do we need to do now? is not saying that you don't know how to coach. It is demonstrating partnership.

- **You try something new that feels uncomfortable**.
  The first time you try something new, it can feel clunky. You might be unsure if it'll be useful. As long as the trigger to use it comes from what the thinker says or does, you'll be surprised how they respond. Trying out a technique with a peer will reduce the feeling of stepping into the unknown. Practice will make you feel more confident when you sense that it's the natural thing to do next. If this is your favourite technique it will be a risk if it is imposed and not co-created. Don't over-explain!

- **You share what you are experiencing**.
  When you offer what you're feeling: *I feel a sense of overwhelm as I listen to what you're saying, how do you feel?*

Sometimes you need to share that you feel stuck. We are learning to notice when we experience something out of the ordinary in our bodies or emotions. Something unusual often comes from what's happening between us or in them. This becomes part of the work together as we become aware of what is happening to us and curious about where it came from. This is sometimes described as using self as an instrument.

- **You invite the thinker to use a metaphor**.
  Metaphors bring unique insights into how someone is thinking, feeling and experiencing their world. When you follow a metaphor together you're in new territory and will have absolutely no idea what you're doing. (They don't work for everyone and can be challenging for some people who are neurodiverse.)

  Simply asking *What does that feel like?* can bring insight. Be cautious, gentle and empathetic about what they discover because it may be intense. Lucia had a session that focused on 'getting rid of the clouds to gain clarity': discussing the clouds one by one, blowing them away and frequently checking in on how the new weather was changing what they sensed and felt.

- **You think you will add more value by speaking – and yet know that not to be true**.
  Your role is to hold the space, not to fill it. Silence is a vital tool in coaching – which is why we have dedicated Chapter 1 to explore it. Sometimes it's all you need. 'To take up space, we must believe in ourselves and the value we add to any activity simply by showing up.'[23]

---

[23] Ibid

TRY THIS WITH A PEER COACH

- Think about which of these examples make you feel most vulnerable.
- Try them out with a peer coach and explore what it is that makes you feel vulnerable.

SIGNS THAT VULNERABILITY ISN'T THERE

A coaching app can ask great questions. A human coach brings vulnerability as well. Coaches straight out of training can rely on buckets of questions and tools that give control, comfort and ideas of what to do next. They make you sound as though you know what you are doing – especially when you feel lost. They protect you from discomfort. And they make you look as though you are not vulnerable. However, it's hard to work in partnership and be seen as fully human when you're picking your questions from a script. When the coach steps into the comfort of familiar questions and tools, the conversation loses flow. Each question can feel disconnected because they come from your thinking rather than the body, mind and spirit of you and the thinker.

Imagine a thinker who explains that they want advice, or where you're unclear whether this is something for therapy. You might be concerned about your code of ethics. Mitigating risk for you to feel safe might sound like setting rules: *Let me explain [tell you!!]. Coaching isn't about me telling you what to do... I am here to do [your explanation of what coaching is].* You have just begun the conversation by telling. When you tell, you lead, and when you lead, they start to follow. Once they are following you it can be difficult to regain partnership. This example looks like teaching. It can also sound like leading, oversharing, talking too much, speaking first, interrupting or choosing what to do next. Too little vulnerability can make the coach seem too big. Partnership is poor when it's all about you. Even when it's not your intention, it can seem like there is no humility here.

Of course, ethical practice requires you to be clear what you can do in coaching and what is outside your remit. Vulnerability requires you to not have that completely pinned down, to hold the not knowing, and avoid jumping into advice or therapy accidentally.

SIGNS THAT THEIR VULNERABILITY IS TOO MUCH

At our first writing retreat in Italy, we met an English-speaking lady in a stationery shop. She was delighted to hear English being spoken. When asked whether she lived locally, within 30 seconds she had tearfully described that she was unhappy because she speaks little Italian and had personal things happening. She was clearly overwhelmed by meeting people with whom she could connect. We could have responded in different ways to this level of vulnerability: ignore it or feel a responsibility to do something. Two days later we were still holding the memory of that encounter. Sometimes vulnerability is so present that it's not the right time to do some work. If you don't know, ask them.

SIGNS THAT OUR VULNERABILITY IS TOO MUCH

Occasionally, you will be too vulnerable to coach today. You might be unwell or something might have happened. Honouring the quality of conversation that people deserve is more important than honouring the commitment you have in the calendar. Sometimes the right thing to do is take care of the relationship and yourself by postponing.

In other contexts, you might not inhabit your physical space or you over-explain questions to make sure they are just right. The thinker picks up the vulnerability and they'll wait for you, carry on without you or keep checking in that you are OK. Sometimes too much vulnerability can accidentally look as though you are too bothered.

Claire had her first conversation with a high-status international customer who looked her in the eye and asked: *How many CEOs have you worked with?* This was her first assignment at this level. In that moment, if she had demonstrated too much vulnerability, the partnership might have been broken and it would have become difficult. Claire knew this might happen and had thought about what to say that would be useful to move from one down. *I work with people who work in organizations like yours, where you are independent and connected to Head Office*, was her reply.

BEING SHOCKED

Imagine someone comes to coaching and shares a recent terminal diagnosis. You're on the receiving end of a vulnerable story that might trigger you. If it has happened to you and you share that, you might risk being the one who is seen. If you choose to focus on it without asking, you have taken the lead. If you move on to not over-sympathize, the thinker might not feel heard. What is likely to happen to you?

There are a few scenarios in coaching where it is worth thinking in advance *What would I do if...?* and this is one of them. How do you receive difficult news as a human and as a coach? They may want to acknowledge and get on with the work they have brought. They may want to vent or process some stuff. You have no idea unless you ask.

As long as it's true for you, imagine saying something like: *If it's useful for you to know, I have something similar in my story. I understand how that is for me and I don't understand how it is for you. [pause] What do we need to do right now?* This creates connection to their story without taking it over with yours. It demonstrates your humanity, reducing the distance between you. They will decide what is most useful in the time you have.

If you don't have a connection with their story, what we like to say is something like: *That's not an experience I've had, and I understand that this must be tough for you. [pause] What do we need to do right now?*

Partnership means being connected enough with one another. Fiona Adamson beautifully describes the 'paradoxical reality' that 'exists in all relationships. We are separate as individuals and we are inextricably connected.'[24] It is this connection that can deepen the work you do together, or limit it. How can you learn to be vulnerable in a way that is genuine and not a place where you leak inappropriately?

LOOK FOR THIS

- Consider what you see that makes you wonder whether someone is vulnerable.
- Ask yourself: *How can I intentionally impact someone else's vulnerability through my own?*

In *Falling Upward*, American priest and writer Richard Rohr describes his journey of vulnerability as a second simplicity:

> If you have forgiven yourself for being imperfect and falling, you can do it now for just about everybody else. If you have not done it for yourself, I am afraid you will likely pass on your sadness, absurdity, judgement and futility to others.[25]

Do you meticulously prepare before a session? Are you terrified if you don't have a plan? Or maybe it's an adrenaline hit? What's the story in your head? (*What if I make it psychologically unsafe for the thinker... and for me? What if they think I'm not worth the money? What if this is the conversation that ruins my reputation or my income stream?*)

Even when conversations feel safe, you still don't have control over the outcome. When you do, it's probably because you are

---

[24] Adamson & Brendgen (2022)
[25] Rohr (2011)

steering it in a way that is comfortable for you, playing your tune, dancing your dance. To truly work in partnership requires both coach and thinker to hold your fear, your performance anxiety, your need to control and to know what's going on, and venture together into the unknown. This is vulnerability.

CHAPTER 5
DISTANCE

Lucia's husband, Marco, is a talented artist. He stands to paint, extending the whole length of his arm with very long brushes. When he is painting an initial sketch, he is fully present with the picture and as far away as he can be from the canvas. The distance gives him an overview of what he is creating. Unless he does that, there is a risk that he will get lost in the details. After a painting session, Marco will ask Lucia to stand back and give him feedback. For him, artful oil painting happens a few brush strokes at a time. When he looks at the brush strokes too closely, they are meaningless spots of colour, but at the right distance they become a beautiful landscape.

WHAT IS DISTANCE?

Like painting, in coaching we need to be at just the right distance to get the essence of what is being communicated. Poet T.S. Eliot uses the words 'neither from nor toward'[1] in one of his poems, which is an eloquent description finding the right distance. When we're too close, we can get lost and become over-curious about the details and facts that interest us. When this is about our curiosity, the thinker does not discover anything new; we are interrogating our own interests and lose connection with the overall picture of what is happening for them.

---

[1] Eliot (1974)

When we are too distant, the thinker can experience a lack of humanity, warmth and connection.

QUESTIONS TO THINK ABOUT

- How do you think about distance in coaching?
- What happens when you cannot hold an appropriate distance?
- What do you do when distance becomes an issue in the room or in the relationship?

WHY APPROPRIATE DISTANCE MATTERS

In an Instagram post describing her relationship with her dad, embodiment practitioner Prentis Hemphill said that 'boundaries are the distance at which I can love you and me simultaneously.'[2] When we navigate it well, distance in coaching co-creates appropriate boundaries that serve both you and the thinker.

These boundaries might cover:

- distance from the system and the work;
- distance from your own emotions;
- distance from the thinker's emotions;
- distance from the story;
- distance from the heart of the work;
- distance from their values;
- distance for safety;
- distance and intimacy;
- distance and difference;
- physical distance from the thinker.

---

[2] Hemphill, Instagram.

DISTANCE FROM THE SYSTEM AND THE WORK

When people start out in coaching, they often find work in places where they've worked before or where they have connections. For many coaches this is where they have credibility. This credibility can turn into paid work. However, knowing the context, or working with a lot of people in the same company, can impact how we manage appropriate distance. This is particularly true for internal coaches.

When you have had interactions with someone or their organization before, your distance is skewed. You may have heard other people talk about them. Your behaviour might be influenced by the assumptions you make and the story you tell yourself about them. You might have already labelled them and be looking for confirmation that you are right. You don't arrive in the room neutral. Just because you worked there before does not mean that you know how it is now.

Distance can become a challenge when you have different assumptions from the thinker about, for example, contact between sessions. If you offer sessional coaching, your style might be to trust them to do the work and not expect much contact in between. If they like to be actively and regularly accountable to you, you may experience your different preferences for distance as a breach of your boundaries. These things simply need a conversation. A coach who offers retained coaching might be a better fit for them, or you might agree that they can send whatever they need to send to you and that you will acknowledge it (and not engage with it). Or you might decide to adapt your fees to cover people having access in between.

DISTANCE FROM YOUR OWN EMOTIONS

However well your boundaries are established, you will sometimes have emotional reactions to what you are seeing, hearing or sensing in the room. You might react or be activated by the thinker. 'Between stimulus and response there is a space. In that space is our power to choose our response. In our response lies our growth and our freedom.'[3] Buddhists call this space between stimulus and response a sacred pause. When you can choose to create this pause, you are more able to keep an appropriate distance from your own emotions.

You can use the pause to be intentional about how you want to use – or not use – what is emerging in you. What is making this particular emotion emerge? Does it allow you to stay neutral and non-judgemental? How could it impact your coaching? What do you want to do with it?

Psychologist Susan David observes that 'to live an intentional and meaningful life you need to develop a critical skill: gain a metaview, the view from above, that broadens your perspective to understand your emotions and how others might be feeling.'[4] Like the artist, when you take a step back to understand how you feel, you can make more conscious choices about how to handle your own emotions in the here and now. This allows you to have a more useful perspective on how you are feeling or reacting.

DISTANCE FROM THE THINKER'S EMOTIONS

We often are on the receiving end of challenging stories, events or struggles that push the people we work with to the edge. Some of the stories are sensitive, some are about obstacles that might seem impossible to overcome. We might bear witness to strong emotions that show up when someone shares their story. The way we respond to these emotions is crucial to create connection. It can impact trust and the depth of the work that we will be able to do next.

Empathy is the most important ingredient to establish that emotional connection in any conversation, not just in coaching. Empathy is defined as our 'ability to share someone else's feelings or experiences by imagining what it would be like to be in that person's

---

[3] Often attributed to neurologist, psychologist and Holocaust survivor Viktor Frankl.
[4] David (2017)

situation.'[5] Brené Brown describes this is as 'feeling with' someone.[6] It is about being curious and kind – whatever emotions show up – and allowing them to know they are not alone in their feelings.[7] Authentic empathy is key to have compassion for others, relate to friends, loved ones, colleagues and complete strangers.

Scientist Paul Zak distinguishes between cognitive and emotional empathy:[8]

- Cognitive empathy is when we are able to put ourselves in someone else's shoes. This is conscious and rational.
- Emotional empathy is about understanding and feeling someone else's emotions. We do this by interpreting what we see, hear, and sense is happening to the other person. This is unconscious and it happens even when we don't share a similar experience.

Cognitive empathy is informed by emotional empathy because our behaviour is driven by the way we react to our own emotions. Psychologist Julia Stietz and her colleagues recognize that 'the peculiarity of empathy is that it enables access to another's internal state by re-creating a representation of that state in the observer.'[9] We need cognitive and emotional empathy in coaching. It's useful to have thought through how we might respond when something unexpected emerges that will shock us. Sharing our experience about what we're hearing is a way to pause and check in with ourselves and what is emerging from the right distance. This might sound like *I'm a little stunned* or *This must be a lot for you to take on*. These interventions also invite the thinker to explore deeper, if it's useful for them.

---

[5] Cambridge Dictionary definition. Available from: https://dictionary.cambridge. org/dictionary/english/empathy. Accessed February 2023.
[6] Brown (2012)
[7] Brown (2018)
[8] Zak (2019)
[9] Stietz et al. (2019)

Insufficient emotional empathy feels like a lack of human connection. Someone won't go deep if it doesn't feel emotionally safe for them to share. If we only bring cognitive empathy in the room, the words we say might be dissonant from our non-verbal communication. This might look like saying *I understand that this is difficult for you* with a monotone voice or crossed arms and legs. It doesn't feel authentic.

We can't be too close either. When we over-empathize or care too much, the thinker can feel swamped. They need to maintain their own personal power. Too much empathy means getting stuck in their distress without moving forward. We could feel overwhelmed or helpless. Or over-identify with their feelings, with the risk of taking them on as our own!

Too much empathy risks being experienced as too much connection. Coaches who describe themselves as empaths, with the ability to sense what others are thinking or feeling, hold a benefit and a costly gift. We need excellent boundaries to avoid absorbing emotion from the thinker. We are the coach; the thinker is the thinker and the work needs to happen in the space between us. Beatrice Zornek says that 'high levels of empathy often come with risks. Like absorbing emotions in the coaching space. We can end up worrying or even digesting emotions on our thinkers' behalf. This is tiring, disempowering and ineffective for the thinker (and ourselves).'[10] We can't be in partnership when the coach appears to be superhuman. 'What you're sensing in your feelings may be very real,' says coach Vanessa Winstanley, 'and it's what you do with that and what meaning you make of it that matters.'[11] Offering not telling is an important skill here. Offer freely with permission and see what lands. What is their reaction to it? And what does that mean for them?

---

[10] Zornek, LinkedIn post.

[11] Winstanley in conversation with 3D Coaching.

QUESTIONS TO THINK ABOUT

- How do you manage to stay at the right distance from your emotions?
- And the thinker's?
- How can you become even more aware of what is emerging in the room?

DISTANCE FROM THE STORY

Italian author and philosopher Niccolò Machiavelli recommended that people who draw landscapes place themselves in the plain to contemplate the nature of the mountains and, in order to contemplate the plains, place themselves upon high mountains.[12] Like the artist and his canvas, keeping the right distance in a conversation means noticing the essence of what is being communicated. We need to be in a place where we can see the overall perspective of the landscape with barely any details.

When people arrive, their initial download of information can sometimes be overwhelming. Some speak for a long time; others barely sketch the picture. When you are listening too closely to the story, you will find yourself lost in the details. Then it's tempting to investigate further. This might not be relevant to the work you need to do today. When you are too distant from the story, you may not be responsive to what the thinker is saying and appear disinterested.

When you are too close, you might dive into the content or the feelings before you're both clear about the work you need to do today. Even if it's a useful question, you're leading because you're choosing to start doing the work when it is not yet agreed between you.

---

[12] Machiavelli (1516)

Coach:	What is your question for today?
Thinker:	I need to move on. I'm not happy with my current employer. There's constant change and it's just too much. I can't keep up with the pace. I've changed my role three times in a year and I'm so confused that I don't know what I'm supposed to do. And, you know what, I've not been asked once what I wanted! This is so frustrating and I feel I'm being treated like a pawn.

When you dive in it might look like this:

Coach:	Wow, three times in a year! I totally understand your frustration. What made you feel like this? [*Past*]
Thinker:	Well, the first role wasn't too bad because I think it was natural career progression, but my new manager was horrible, such a control freak! I didn't really feel he trusted me. In the second role, things got even worse because I stayed with the same manager but moved to a new team and I didn't really feel I was welcome there... [*Coach has new insights, thinker does not*]
Coach:	I see. What would you like to achieve in this session?
Thinker:	I'd like to think about my next step.
Coach:	Next step?
Thinker:	Yes, if I should leave or try to stay. But I'm not really sure.
Coach:	What have you tried so far to stay? [*Past*]
Thinker:	[*Continues with a story about his past for the next 10 minutes*]

Coaching is future focused. Leading the thinker into the past has increased the distance from the agreed outcome of the session. Here is a more appropriate distance for the second question:

Coach:	Too much change and no voice in it? Wow!
Thinker:	Yes, you see what I'm saying? If they treat me like this it means I'm not being valued. I feel like a fraud.
Coach:	A fraud?
Thinker:	[*Looks down silently, then back at the coach*]
Coach:	What are you noticing as you say that? [*Present*]
Thinker:	I'm tired of feeling like this. [*Silence*]
Coach:	And today, what do we need to do?
Thinker:	Change it?
Coach:	What would you like to feel different by the end of our time together?
Thinker:	I'd like to feel myself again because I don't. I keep thinking about how much effort I put into what I do and, you know, I feel like my self-confidence is at stake here. I don't like it!
Coach:	And in 15 minutes' time how will you know you're a bit more yourself?
Thinker:	I'll feel lighter, I'll feel passionate about what I do. I'd have the courage to speak to my manager and try to say what I think instead of hiding.
Coach:	Lighter? More passionate? More courageous?
Thinker:	Yes!
Coach:	And how will you know we've done that?
Thinker:	This weight in my stomach will disappear.
Coach:	What do we need to talk about to get rid of this weight?
Thinker:	I think why I lack confidence in this relationship and what I can do to change it.

This time, the coach offers the highlights of what they're hearing: *Too much change and no voice?* Their tone is an invitation to go deeper. The conversation moves away from the detail of the story (the past) and becomes about personal transformation (the present and the future). The coach manages to keep an appropriate distance to hold an overview instead of getting focused on the past.

The first coach interrogates the problem and stays in the past. They might be looking for a solution in their head or thinking of similar situations they have experienced. When the thinker is very talkative, it is easy to get lost in the problem instead of exploring with the person what they can actually change.

The second coach speaks to the person, trying to work out with them what will move the situation forward. This is present and future. The exploration is about how the thinker feels and how they want to feel different in the relationship with his manager. The thinker moves forward just a few minutes after the start.

When we are too close to the story, we can find ourselves focusing on the past. It is possible to keep an appropriate distance by facing the future even when they speak about the past: *As you hear yourself say that, what do you notice?* is a question that encourages the thinker to stay in the here and now.

Another useful question to avoid getting too close to the story is to ask yourself: *Who will gain an insight from this question?* If it's you, ask a different question!

TRY THIS WITH A PEER COACH

If you want to find an appropriate distance from the story, try **blind coaching** with a peer. This is when you ask the thinker not to tell you anything about the story. Instead use closed questions to work out what you're doing: *Are you clear in your head what the question is you want to explore today?* Keep asking closed questions about the work. They will do almost all their thinking on the inside. Watch and sense, and offer a question only when it's useful: *Was that an insight?*

DISTANCE FROM THE HEART OF THE WORK

Working on tasks can create easy wins, and it's the deeper human work that creates sustainable change. That is the heart of the work of coaching. When you are too close, or spend too much time in the story, you might end up colluding and not notice where the challenge might be. The closer you get to the heart of the challenge, the deeper you can go together. This is where real transformation can happen.

It's not your responsibility to find the heart of the challenge. The thinker will find it when you let them do the work. If you were the coach listening to the thinker in the last example, here are some of the things you might notice and explore to help them go deeper:

- **What sounds different**
  These could be strong statements; single words that are repeated several times or with a different tone from the rest of the sentence, like *It is not fair* or *I'm being treated like a pawn.* Offering back single words as a question helps them listen to themselves.

- **What looks dissonant**
  Perhaps they raised an eyebrow every time they talked about their manager (without even realizing it).

- **With an invitation**
  Shall we go deeper? or *And if we went deeper here...?*

- **With an observation**
  This is the third time you have said that you feel uncomfortable or *Every time you say you love your job, you shake your head.*

When you mirror cues or energy shifts, or play back meaningful words, you open the door to evoke new awareness. You don't need to say much. One word can be enough. And then you need to hold your nerve and stay silent while they travel deeper into their learning.

DISTANCE FROM THEIR VALUES

A friend of Lucia's – let's call him Carlo – secretly confessed he'd betrayed his fiancée. Lucia still remembers that moment:

> I was frozen. I could feel a battle going on inside me between two dominant voices. The judge in me was shouting *Are you serious? How could you do that?* The friend in me said *I get it! There are moments when I'm not myself too and I do things that I wish I could erase the moment after they happen. How can I help you now?* I had to choose if I wanted to be the judge or the friend before I could lower the voices in my head.

When Carlo told Lucia his secret, he was overwhelmed. He trusted Lucia to keep his secret safe. He needed to be heard and feel understood. He needed support and empathy. Lucia was unprepared. Carlo shared something in conflict with Lucia's values.

In coaching, we might have conversations where there is a clash of values or beliefs. How you respond will impact trust and rapport. Sometimes you will have to withdraw from the work because the distance between your values or beliefs and theirs is too big for one or both of you. Of course, if you have explored the question of distance yourself and decided you can continue, you will still need to explore this with them.

QUESTIONS TO THINK ABOUT

Imagine working with someone who has a very different set of values from you.

- What would be your attitude towards that person?
- How difficult could it be to stay neutral and non-judgemental?
- What would make you decide to stop the work?

DISTANCE FOR SAFETY

As an organizational coach, Lucia worked in very competitive and fast-paced organizations, where people were under constant pressure. Their behaviours were often driven by a fight/flight/freeze reaction. When they were tired or stressed, their negative energy spread. They were less able to reflect on how to respond to what they perceived as threats. This made that workplace toxic. She used to imagine that she was wearing a waterproof raincoat that protected her from the behaviour of people around her and their feelings. She chose to put in some distance for safety.

What do you do to keep your distance from toxic work environments?

DISTANCE AND INTIMACY

Coaching is an unusual profession. You learn deep truths from the people you coach and they don't learn very much at all about you. You will feel very connected to some and less to others. A level of intimacy, or connection, is necessary to build trust. And too much intimacy brings other dilemmas. Emotional distance is an ethical issue. How close can you get?

Some coaches never share personal information. Others are happy to disclose where they went on holiday or that it is their child's birthday.

It can be disturbing or exciting to hear someone say, *You know me better than my partner does.* Remember that this relationship is not normal – we are talking deeply. And only about them. Coaching means that two people are likely to become close over time. This is proximity which is natural. And 'we like things and people more as they become more familiar to us. This is known as the mere exposure effect. The "propinquity effect" refers to people's tendency to form bonds, friendships, romantic relationships with people they see frequently.'[13]

____

[13] Gordon (2022)

Proximity is about more than the boundary between professionalism and romance. Sometimes, not always, closeness can cause you to collude and lose the challenging edge of coaching. You can move from what John Blakey describes as the high challenge, high support 'loving boot' where the work happens and find yourselves in 'cosy' conversations.[14] Who on your list needs to be moved from someone who pays you, to someone you have lunch with, or don't work with anymore? This can be a difficult boundary to negotiate when you both have a vested interest in continuing the professional relationship. This is another place where supervision is useful.

QUESTIONS TO THINK ABOUT

- Where do you sense-check your ethical boundaries?
- What are your boundaries about being known?
- How will you know if you are too close?
- Is it OK to share a coffee or a glass of wine with a thinker? Whatever you think, some coaches will hold the opposite view. Knowing that, what are the ethical questions which you need to hold here?

DISTANCE AND DIFFERENCE

Karen Bruns has worked on identifying cognitive biases that can affect the way we coach.[15] [16] She and Lucia have identified some that impact the way we hold distance in coaching. Others have been explored in other chapters.

---

[14] Blakey & Day (2012)

[15] All the references to bias in this chapter come from Karen Bruns's work. Available from: https://monarchcoachingllc.com

[16] Cognitive biases. Available from: https://en.wikipedia.org/wiki/List_of_cognitive_biases. Accessed August 2023.

- **Affinity bias** happens when you connect with others who share similar interests and backgrounds.[17] This can make you too close – talking about what you have in common or liking them because they share your passions, experiences or origins. What needs to happen for you not to collude? And how do you build connection with someone who comes from a very different background, country of origin, religion, sexuality, etc?
- **Beauty bias** happens when, for example, you believe that attractive people are more successful, competent and qualified. Imagine coaching a well-known leader who inspires you for their competence and confidence. They too are human. And you need to be normal for them to be able to demonstrate their humanity and vulnerability.

QUESTIONS TO THINK ABOUT

- Which of these biases is the greatest risk for you?
- What impact does it have on your coaching?
- What needs to shift in you to hold the right distance?

PHYSICAL DISTANCE FROM THE THINKER

The COVID-19 pandemic made the world more sensitive than ever to space and distance. During lockdowns, a two metre distance in a conversation with a masked stranger might have felt disconnected for some. And yet an unmasked conversation close up could feel overwhelming to someone who had been shielding. There are cultural, emotional and even medical norms that mean what is too close for one person is distant for another.

---

[17] Builtin. Available from: https://builtin.com/diversity-inclusion/unconscious-bias-examples. Accessed August 2023.

When proximity feels uncomfortable, in that moment someone who is able to access their personal power can move a little to make the distance feel more comfortable. Claire can think of a couple of people she has known socially who move closer after she has moved back to restore a comfortable distance. This feels deeply uncomfortable.

While most – but not all – people negotiate physical space and distance intuitively, in conversation you can't do that so easily. The online coach leans close into the camera. The face-to-face coach sits very near to the thinker. There will always be a way you can change the distance even in a small way.

Too close might also relate to sounds – too many 'oohs' and 'ahhs'. It might reflect an over-caring mindset. Online, too detached can happen when the coach is in the centre of the screen. You look like a newsreader or a manager. Sitting slightly at an angle off-centre can be experienced as less telling and more engaging. Face to face, too much distance might be about the position of the chairs, or indeed how formal or informal you are. Distance and proximity impact trust.

Claire invites people to stand if they want to. She stands too (otherwise the physical and power distance is too big). Once you are standing, you can both move and that enables them to modify how close or how far apart you are, which direction you are each facing and more. Online, it's not unusual for us to stand and to move to the edge of the camera as the thinker flows with the work.

The responsibility to negotiate and renegotiate the distance or closeness that serves your work needs to be explicit and will be different in every conversation. Otherwise, you're making all the decisions about what is and what is not useful. That's not partnership.

If you watch recordings of dialogues with no sound, even films, it can be enlightening to see how much you communicate your desire to jump in – or the opposite – through your distance from someone else.

- How close to the camera do you sit when you are online? If you are 40 cm from your camera, or closer, and they are that close to theirs, there is very little space between you. Moving back and inviting them to move back can change the dynamic.
- Leaning towards the thinker on screen or in person has the opposite effect and reduces the space between you. It also makes you look bigger.
- Your facial expressions can have the same impact as leaning in – you look as though you are about to speak.
- Putting your hand up has a similar impact.

When the distance between you and the thinker is small, it reduces the space they need to think.

QUESTIONS TO THINK ABOUT

- What do you notice about physical distance in person or about distance from the screen when online?
- How much do you prefer to be close or far away?
- What impact could you make if you demonstrated distance differently?

HOW TO CALIBRATE DISTANCE

The first time Claire met coach and trainer John Whittington he was constellating, or mapping out, coffee mugs to get a sense of how close or far away he needed to be from various relationships in an upcoming stakeholder meeting.[18] He was looking at more than physical distance. It was a sense-check about where he fitted in the system. Mapping can be a useful way of exploring distance and proximity in any of the examples we have described here. If another

---

[18] Whittington (2020)

perspective is useful to help you see more clearly, a supervisor or peer coach will be able to work with you.

Perhaps there is another more intimate aspect of distance. The distance we take in order to be able to do this work. 'Every day, you need to make yourself radically unavailable so that when you are with people you can be fully present,' says author Shaun Lambert.[19]

LOOK FOR THIS

Think about two of the people you coach – one that you love to work with and one where you have less energy.

- Think about some of the distance we have talked about in this chapter.
- Then ask yourself: *What do I notice about distance when I'm working with each person?*

Distance and proximity are things that you may think of intuitively, or barely notice until something happens that brings it to your attention. It can take humility and courage to do your own work and the insights you can gain about distance from reflective practice and supervision are invaluable for your work and your psychological safety.

---

[19] Lambert (2014)

CHAPTER 6
COURAGE AND INSIGHT

One day, coach Gary Crotaz had a moment of clarity that he needed to leave his organization.[1] He left a sticky note on his boss's desk saying *I'm leaving,* not knowing when or how. The insight required an enormous amount of courage if it was to become a real tangible action and not a pipe dream. He calls these life-changing moments of insight 'sticky note moments'.

Courage and insight are qualities that are needed in both coach and thinker for new insights and transformational change to happen. A lack of courage in one or both of you can make conversations feel transactional. You can accidentally keep them in what they know already. 'We can choose courage, or we can choose comfort, but we can't have both. Not at the same time,' says Brené Brown.[2] Too much courage, or too much of a distance between your courage in the room and theirs in their situation can make you reckless or fearful.

WHY COURAGE MATTERS

Fear is a normal feeling. Brené Brown describes it as 'a negative, short-lasting high-alert emotion in response to a perceived threat'[3]; like going into a coaching conversation that you are being paid to deliver, without a plan, or coaching someone who you perceive to have more personal power or status than you do. 'Fear,' says Alistair

---

[1] Crotaz, *The Unlock Moment podcast.*
[2] Brown (2015b)
[3] Brown (2021)

Bradley, 'or the converse boredom means we cannot be in flow. Flow is where we are stretched and capable. Sometimes we have to have the courage and the vulnerability to change our belief about the challenge and sometimes we need to be honest and say, "I am not the right coach right now.'"[4]

You can conceal your fear behind control, or learn to embrace it, acknowledge it and use it. You are doing deep work together. The thinker may have some fear. You both need courage. Courage comes when you draw on the strength you have to keep going in spite of the fear. It 'starts with showing up and letting ourselves be seen,' says Brené Brown.[5] Every time you step into a coaching conversation, you need courage. If there isn't a tiny bit of wondering how it will be today, you may have been working with this person for too long. If you truly enter the room with no agenda and a willingness to do whatever is needed today, there will always be a small element of fear. And adrenaline.

Your courage is the catalyst for their insight. That is not enough. They also need courage to do the work.

WHAT COURAGE FEELS LIKE FOR US

Courage in coaching means that we are managing and regulating our own emotion at the same time as supporting the thinker to do some deep work. Saying what we see without judgement is a key skill in coaching and requires courage to speak out.

Fear in us often emerges right at the beginning of the conversation as the thinker starts exploring what they are bringing:

- I have worked with three or four coaches on this before. I'm still stuck, so I thought I'd come to you.
- I've been thinking about this day and night for a week.

---

[4] Bradley in conversation with 3D Coaching.

[5] Brown (2015a)

- I haven't been able to find a way forward with this for more than 20 years. (Claire really heard that from the person she was coaching for an observed credential exam.)

A natural, being-professional response is to feel the pressure of the expectation and say nothing. They've been working on this for a long time (*What if I don't shift it either?*). The pressure starts ticking like an unexploded bomb. It's taking a little of your attention all the time. The further you get into the work, and the less progress they make, the more you worry that you're making things worse. Now it has become about your anxiety, performance, competence or value.

Courage means naming the pressure straight away before it turns from their fact into your fear: *What do we need to do differently today so that...:*

- we can find enough of a way forward with this?
- you can sleep tonight?
- you're not thinking about it for the next 20 years?

It takes courage to be that direct. Now we can work in partnership and share the responsibility from the start. The time bomb has disappeared and you can focus on being present. Claire's daughter Lucy has a new coach who asked in their first session: *What might I do that will disappoint you?* That's courage!

If you want the people you work with to be courageous, you need courage too. 'Courage is contagious,' says Brené Brown. 'A critical mass of brave leaders is the foundation of an intentionally courageous culture. Every time we are brave with our lives, we make the people around us a little braver and our organizations bolder and stronger.'[6]

---

[6] Brown (2018)

It takes courage to:

- **Say what you see**
  You've suddenly stopped talking about the past and you're now looking at the future with a different energy. What happened?
- **Offer what you sense**
  I'm wondering what belief you're holding when you stay away from having that difficult conversation.
- **Confront**
  And as you tell the story of why you won't manage to get to this ambitious goal, what's real and what's a barrier that you've built for yourself?
- **Encourage risk-taking**
  I understand that starting a business can be scary, but what's the worst thing that could happen if it fails?
- **Offer honest feedback**
  I'm noticing a lack of progress here and am wondering if this is still a priority for you?
- **Share what you experience**
  I'm feeling tension in my body as I hear your story. What's happening for you?
- **Push**
  What could get you even closer to your goal?
- **Charge fees**

Transformational coaching takes courage. You manage your fear, take risks, say what you see and use your intuition to serve the thinker's agenda and goals. Fear drives a lot of the human behaviours that get in our way: we are afraid of breaking trust, checking in, losing the work, not bringing value, losing control or pushing them too hard.

Courage requires vulnerability. This may come from our own experience of seeing it done badly – with aggression or judgement. In French, the root of the word challenge is accusation. If I challenge, am I being disloyal? What if it breaks trust? Will they accept it? If challenge is going to be useful, we will risk breaking trust. That makes us vulnerable.

TRY THIS

The coaching room might not be the place to exercise your courage muscle.

- Do something that makes you feel vulnerable and out of control – one coach put on headphones and went and danced in the park – you will have your own ideas. Ask social media if you need ideas (that will also take courage).

WHAT COURAGE FEELS LIKE FOR THEM

Before we think about the thinker's courage, we acknowledge that not everyone who comes to coaching wants to do work. That might be because:

- they have been sent;
- they are unaware of the benefit of coaching;
- this is the wrong time or place;
- you are not the right coach;
- they regularly talk about this thing and never quite get to action ;
- they are not courageous enough to do the work they know needs to be done.

CHECKING HOW MUCH COURAGE THEY HAVE TODAY

Lucia recounts the courage her husband had as a child when he spent his summers playing with his cousins:

Their dads built tree houses in the garden. Some of the older children climbed higher into the top of the trees until they could see the sea. They connected the crowns with ropes: one to walk and one to hold. They then used the tightrope to walk from one tree to the other by holding on to branches, when there were some, or to the 'safety' rope when there was nothing else to hold on to. Every step took courage. And there was a point where they had to continue because they couldn't go back.

We get to this point in every challenging coaching conversation. We have to walk on a rope and it is wobbly, unsafe and scary. We don't know what to do. What if we screw things up? The art is to manage our fear and stay grounded in our presence. They will work it out. Only if we hold the challenge will real transformation happen.

Agreeing at the start of a session or coaching relationship how much challenge someone is comfortable with is not enough. You still don't know if they have enough courage for the question you are about to ask. It's useful to gradually ask permission during the conversation: *Can I challenge here?* If you're unclear about how much courage they have left, another useful question might be: *If I was to be challenging right now, I would be asking...* or indeed *How much courage do you have left today?*

SIGNS THAT COURAGE ISN'T THERE

Without your courage, people might still have insights. Things become clearer as they talk through their challenge. If they come with confused ideas, they leave with a better understanding of what is happening and what they need to address to resolve it. Psychologist Sidney Jourard explains that 'no [person] can come to know [themselves] except as the outcome of disclosing [themselves] to another.'[7]

---

[7] Jourard (1972)

With your courage and without theirs, no real transformation can happen. You end up doing most of the work. They need courage to go deeper, to challenge their own assumptions and beliefs, to move to action. Otherwise there will be no real progress and you will notice this across sessions. When this happens, it takes courage for you to say, *I'm noticing we seem stuck, what is the work we really need to be doing here?*

QUESTIONS TO THINK ABOUT

Think of a time you coached someone where you did not observe courage.
- What did you feel?
- What did you notice that you did not share?
- Without fear, what would you have done differently?

INSIGHT

Insight is '(the ability to have) a clear, deep, and sometimes sudden understanding of a complicated problem or situation.'[8] We see or sense in a way that unlocks new awareness that enables forward action.

Before Lucia became a coach, she sometimes wished she had the ability to see people's deepest fears and desires, hopes and dreams, and their hidden motivations. She dreamed of using this to see into people's hearts, help them see the truth about themselves and guide them on their own journeys of self-discovery. Later, she realized that the most useful insight in coaching is the thinker's insight into their stuff. Coaching is not any kind of psychological analysis. Be careful whose insight we are facilitating through our questions.

---

[8] Cambridge Dictionary definition. Available from: https://dictionary.cambridge. org/dictionary/english/insight. Accessed August 2023.

WHY INSIGHT MATTERS

Artful coaching is about the quality of the insight that emerges for the thinker much more than the beauty or fluency of your questions. It is the depth of their insight that moves coaching from transactional to transformational. 'Insights are always the precursor to sustainable behaviour change,' says Michael Bungay Stanier.[9]

Facilitating someone to see things differently is a more effective way to help them discover who they are and how they can be successful than telling them. Physician Gabor Maté says:

> That is why knowledge and insight have the power to transform, and why insight is more helpful to people than advice. If we gain the ability to look into ourselves with honesty, compassion and with unclouded vision, we can identify the ways we need to take care of ourselves. We can see the areas of the self formally hidden in the dark.[10]

This is like holding up a mirror so the thinker sees something new for themselves. You notice and pay attention to the small details that they don't see or sense. You offer them back so they can notice, dig deeper and make meaning. You can only develop this art when you are fully present and listening to the thinker.

Gary, at the start of this chapter, had the courage to take action from the insight that he needed to leave. The first insight, *I must leave*, led to an action: the sticky note. This line between what was and what would emerge opened the possibility for new insights. It takes courage to cross the line and look something in the eye. Encouraging thinkers to cross the line to evoke new insight might be:

---

9 Bungay Stanier (2020)
10 Mate (2011)

- You're unclear whether to stay in this role or leave. Can I invite you to stand up and step outside that door. Imagine that you have decided to leave. How does that feel?
- Imagine that person is here right now – tell them what you need to say.

WHAT YOU DO WITH THE THINKER'S RESPONSE

It takes courage to share observations: you find the opportunity to say what you see, hear or notice and then wait to see what happens. When you offer, you demonstrate you are paying attention and are genuinely interested and invested in their development. This can build trust and strengthen the relationship. On the other hand, if your observations are not well received, you might fear that this will erode trust. The fear of being wrong means you miss the opportunity for them to generate new insight. You don't even take the risk.

You can see when insights are emerging. They might look away. Your observation was a little push that has kept their thinking in flow and they are moving forward. You are curious to talk about what they're learning and to co-create an action plan that will take them closer to where they want to be. You are ready to move on. They are still processing. You need to wait.

This is the moment where we often see coaches rushing. It is the moment you have been waiting for. Let it happen. You will need some questions to consolidate the learning. And if you ask them too quickly, the transformation might never come.

WAYS OF EVOKING INSIGHT

The most useful way to evoke insight is to notice it's happening and not to walk over it. Even when someone has a life-changing insight, it's not unusual for both the coach and thinker to miss it. It can get lost in the words or the sound of the conversation. We will talk more about this in Part II. 'What this really means,' says Michael Bungay Stanier, 'is being relentless: staying curious long enough to allow the other person to create the insight and space to reach the heart of the matter.'[11]

Your role is to watch them getting the insight, not to ask what they know already and try to work out what insights you think they need to see. When you are thinking or analysing, flow is lost.[12] If you want to stay away from interpreting, your language is about offering what you see rather than making your own meaning of what you see, hear or sense.

Table 1 shows a few examples of how coaches with different levels of skill might share the same gut feelings.

Table 1: Sharing gut feelings

Situation	Interpretation	Observation	Comment
Loud emotion	You seem angry now!	I notice you changed your tone of voice as you talked about this?	One labels the thinker's feelings that are not his own. The other notices the change of tone as an offer.
The thinker gets quieter and sounds like they are hesitating	What makes you anxious?	I'm wondering if you're hesitating?	One interprets the change of pace. The other has shared what they heard as a question.
'There's this and this and this and also that and that and that' (without taking a breath)	You are very overwhelmed!	What do you notice as you say those things?	One comes up with a diagnosis. The other facilitates the thinker's self-discovery.

---

[11] Bungay Stanier (2020)
[12] Bradley in conversation with 3D Coaching.

Deep stuff is coming up	What relaxes you?	Wow, I feel tension in my body as I hear this!	One labels a solution (relax) and leads the conversation to a more comfortable place. The other uses what they sense in their body to invite more exploration.

As you can see from Table 1, it is important to talk about what you sense as much as you can and follow up with the thinker's exploration as they search for an answer inside themselves. They will discover what is happening, which will lead to new awareness.

LOOK FOR THIS

Consider these questions to help you reflect on the last coaching session you had:

- What did you do that evoked new insight in the thinker?
- What did you see, hear or sense that made you wonder whether new insight was emerging for them?
- What will you do again, or differently, next time?

WHAT YOU SENSE: YOUR INTUITION AND HOW YOU USE IT

Everyone has preferences about how they notice. Learning how to engage different senses can deepen your work so that you pay attention to what you feel as well as what you think. Coaching is a mindful conversation: intentionally focusing your attention in the present and noticing what you see, hear and sense.

When you turn down the thinking in your head and also focus on what is happening in you as you listen to the thinker, you offer your humanity. Noticing and sharing what you sense or feel is happening in your body in the moment can serve their learning. Bringing your body into the space has a significant impact on how you work in partnership. This is what is meant by using your body as an instrument. If this feels uncomfortable, it's worth doing some work – because it will be impacting the conversation even when that is not your intention.

Intuition is a form of sensing that is a superpower and a risk. It can bring insight for the thinker. Or it can be used by the coach to lead and chase a hypothesis. Focusing trainer Ann Weiser Cornell talks about sensing in two different ways:[13]

- A felt sense that is freshly forming right here right now – a deep wondering.
- A feeling that comes from your wisdom or experience – she calls this intuition something that you know implicitly without pausing, for example, like a teacher knowing how to calm down a room of excited children.

You get to know people well over time and might have a gut feeling about the reasons behind their thinking or behaving. Your intuition is a hunch, something you noticed that stands out that might be useful to share. Intuitions are subjective because they come from data you have interpreted through your own lenses instead of mirroring back what you see from a more neutral stance; you might be wrong.

Intuition has the potential to create new learning and can be a powerful catalyst to evoke new awareness. 'Intuition demands presence and everything human without evaluating to bring forward a useful question.'[14] So, how do you stay away from interpreting instead of offering?[15]

---

[13] Weiser Cornell, *Focusing Tip #792*.

[14] Bradley in conversation with 3D Coaching.

[15] Baldelli, *Coaching Outside the Box*.

Here are some questions you could ask yourself before you offer:

- What purpose is offering this intuition serving?
- How do I stay away from interpreting what I sense?

If your intuition is serving the work you are here to do and not your desire to lead in your preferred direction, then you are on the right track.

WHAT CAN STOP INSIGHT

You stop insight when you don't see it or speak before the thinker has finished thinking. Note taking is the most common way to miss insight because you are looking away. The moment you take your eyes off the thinker, you are missing something. Your presence is impacted by the need to write and remember.

Lucia worked with an aspiring coach who was typing notes. She was looking at the document on the screen, not at the thinker. The click of the keyboard was louder than the thinker's voice. There were three players in the conversation: the coach, the thinker and the laptop.

As you realize there is no need to remember, you will see the amount of notes you take decreasing over time. We have reduced the notes we take to around three or four words in a session. The best questions come in response to what you have just heard. Patterns will emerge repeatedly, so it will be easy to spot them and offer them back. You only need to remember what you are doing in this session and how they will know you have done it. You can write that down without taking your eyes off the thinker. Sometimes you might add a few keywords that you might go back to. That's enough.

TRY THIS WITH A PEER COACH

Have a coaching conversation without taking any notes at all. Then debrief with your peer coach.
- How did you feel?
- What did you notice?
- What surprised you?
- What impact did no notes have on how they experienced your presence?

WHAT IF THERE IS NO INSIGHT

There can be an adrenaline rush when a thinker gets an insight. You might see it as a measure of your work, maybe your value? It can look like a light has switched on in their head. You both worked hard for this moment. For many coaches, seeing insight is the most rewarding part of the work.

You will not witness big shifts in every session. Sometimes they make such a small step forward that you can barely appreciate it. Then you start panicking, *My approach didn't work*. Even worse, you might ask them if they made any progress, and sound like you are asking *Was I any good today?*

When transformation happens, coaching is like a chemical reaction. The change is permanent and nothing is the same afterwards.[16] They will keep moving forward with their thinking after the session. When you are not sure they had insight, stay positive: *Have you made any progress?* becomes *What progress have you made today?* Sometimes the subject might feel enormous at the beginning and you wonder whether you will be able to make meaningful progress. In this case, manage expectations by asking *What will it look like when we have moved this forward a little, by the end of today's session?*

---

[16] Pedrick (2020)

The insight may not come in the room at all. We have worked with people who start their conversation a couple of days before they meet us and arrive with their insight 90% formed. They only need to talk until they have made a small movement. Others will get the insight an hour or a day after we have finished the session, as long as we end well. Claire worked with someone who would do all the work the day before their session and use the conversation to report back. It took them both a while to realize that this is also transformational coaching. It just looks different. They said that they would not have done the processing if they had not known they were meeting their coach.

HOW TO TAKE THIS TO THE NEXT LEVEL

Many growing coaches struggle with sharing observations. This skill requires some of the qualities we describe here. You can't be courageous without letting go of control. This needs empathy and vulnerability. Beginner coaches rarely manage to focus their attention on what is happening beyond the words. Their conversations focus on hearing the problem and they don't notice the thinker with their eyes.

Experienced coaches look for dissonance and resonance, noticing what is being communicated non-verbally, and exploring emotions. You won't always know what to do with what you see, hear or sense. We have heard coaches say, *I noticed it but I wasn't sure when to share it and then I lost the opportunity: it was too late.* You noticed, you processed the new information, and held on to it instead of offering it back immediately. This impacts your presence because you are busy wondering what to do with it.

Artful coaches focus on what is happening at a human level. Now you mostly say what you see and avoid interpretation because you tend to focus on observable data that can reveal new insight for the thinker. Artful coaching is as risky as improv, where artists like Pippa Evans play in front of large audiences:

> When you are fully present with someone... looking at everything in front of you and listening to everything that is being said – you have so much information that what you want to do next – what you need to do next – becomes so clear.[17]

That is when the insight pops up.

QUESTIONS TO THINK ABOUT

- What do you do to bring the right amount of courage to the room?
- How does your courage change depending on who you are coaching?
- What needs to change in you for you to be able to consistently demonstrate more courage?

It takes courage to demonstrate courage and requires many of the qualities we have described in Part I. It can take courage to be silent when someone is paying you. Holding your not-knowing nerve is an art that takes practice. You need humility to take appropriate risks that can leave you feeling exposed and vulnerable as you try and negotiate an appropriate distance between you and the thinker, and the work you are doing together. All these qualities create an environment where you can work in partnership and where someone feels truly heard and gets new insights into their own stuff. That is artful coaching.

---

[17] Evans (2021)

PART 2
HUMANITY BETWEEN

The human qualities explored in Part I can be seen in the space between us:

- Partnership
- The dance
- The words
- The music
- Trust

If you want to see what this looks like in your coaching, there are some ideas in Chapter 12, **Using recordings**, for reflective practice. If you want to explore this more deeply, mentor coaching is a useful place to go. A mentor will watch recordings of your coaching with you.

CHAPTER 7
PARTNERSHIP

It's not technical skill that differentiates a good coach from an artful one. It's the combination of competence and humanity that enables partnership. This can be seen in the dance and heard in the music of the conversation. You trust each other and trust the process. Partnership is an ethical practice, which emerges as you co-create the work together.

Coaching is a dialogue. William Isaacs describes this as:

> a shared inquiry of thinking and reflecting together. It is not something you do **to** another person, it is something you do **with** people. Indeed a large part of this learning has to do with learning to shift your attitude about relationships with others, so that we gradually give up the effort to make them understand us and come to a greater understanding of ourselves and each other.[1]

Coaches need to do less 'efforting' and more sharing. Coaching can only be a partnership when you share decisions about how you work together each and every time you meet. This requires all the qualities we have described so far: silence, a willingness to not know, humility, vulnerability, appropriate distance and courage. 'Ambiguity exists even when the formal roles seem clear,' wrote Ed

---

[1] Isaacs (1999); emphasis added.

Schein. 'This mutual ignorance is rarely acknowledged explicitly.'[2] To work in partnership, we need to be explicit about what we are doing.

It's a lack of partnership that makes a recording of a session sound like the coach and thinker are stumbling over each other. You can see and hear that they aren't in flow. They have lost connection.

PARTNERSHIP IS UNIQUE

'Within each person is the miracle of a unique consciousness unlike any other in the universe,' says influencer Bryant McGill.[3] You have no idea how to have a useful conversation with this person in this place at this time. And when you do know, you won't know whether the work you are doing together is having the impact that they hope or intend *unless you ask them*. Growing coaches tend to work too hard, think too hard, ask too much, take too much in, analyse too much, want to understand too much and want too much to be resolved.

Partnership underpins the work you do together. You can't make the decision about what you are doing and how you will work together once, for the whole coaching relationship. You will need to negotiate every time you meet. Each space and time are different from the last time you had an encounter. Until you get some clarity about what you are doing together today, you will remain in Ed Schein's 'mutual ignorance'. You work in partnership when you have constant negotiation throughout every conversation about how you need to work together today, and every time you meet.

Coach Carly Anderson says, 'partnering is characterized most simply by allowing the client to choose what happens next, throughout the session.'[4] Without this invitation, you are leading.

When professional coaching bodies use words like contracting, designing a working alliance and re-contracting, they describe:

- the business agreement, terms and conditions;

---

2 Schein (2009)
3 McGill (2012)
4 Anderson (2015)

- fees, how many sessions, etc;
- the things you have agreed to work on over time;
- the work you are doing today.

These are very different tasks. Some are logistical and others are about the work in the room. Clarity can make it simpler. We use:

- contracting and re-contracting to describe the logistics;
- rightsizing and checking in for the things we do in every conversation.

THINK ABOUT

- How important is partnership for you at the moment?
- What do you do to intentionally create it?
- How do you know that there is partnership in the room?

RIGHTSIZING

Partnership is not catching a list of bullet points or coming up with an agenda. Nor is it asking for feedback on your performance as a coach. It is about negotiating together what is the work for today, how you're going to do it and how you'll know you have done it. When this is clear enough, you have an agreement or indeed agree that you don't know what you are doing or where you are heading. This establishes the partnership today. You have made the work the right size for the time you have today. This is described in detail in *Simplifying Coaching*.[5]

Early in her coaching career, Lucia was coaching someone with a challenge that resonated with her. Lucia had gone through a similar situation and knew exactly where they would go, thought she felt what they felt, and had experienced what they were going

---

[5] Pedrick (2020)

through. She could have thought she had the recipe for a successful conversation. Instead she asked, *What do we need to discuss on this topic for you to achieve your goal today?* What came back was incredibly different from what Lucia expected. Without rightsizing, she would have led the thinker where she thought it was useful to go. It was essential to **co-create the container** for the thinker's learning. You are in partnership when you have agreed what you are doing before you dive into the part of their story that most interests you.

Coach Marion Franklin offers two crucial questions to hold in your mind, while listening to the thinker's story, that will keep you in partnership, and in dialogue with the human not the problem:[6]

- *Why are they telling me this?* connects you to the person and what they are experiencing, and keeps you away from talking about the problem.
- *What's making this a problem for this person?* makes you curious about the relationship that the thinker uniquely has with this challenge and stops you from making assumptions and projecting what you might experience in a similar situation.

These enable you to go deeper. And it is artful coaching.

WHO MAKES THE MEANING?

People come to coaching as a safe place where they can be open and honest without fear of judgement. They may not know why they have come. You offer them a place to feel seen and heard and gain new insights into their own stuff so that they move forward in their thinking.[7] This is a place for *them* to make sense and meaning. When ICF updated their coaching competencies in 2021, 'creating awareness' was renamed 'evokes awareness'.[8] This is good news

---

6 Franklin (2019)

7 Pedrick (2020)

8 ICF Core Competencies (2019)

because you can't create awareness. New insight only comes when the thinker sees their situation in a different way.

Sense-making, say academics Weick, Sutcliffe and Obstfeld, is 'the activity that enables us to turn the ongoing complexity of the world into a "situation that is comprehended explicitly in words and that serves as a springboard into action".[9] That's an external process that you can facilitate. Meaning-making comes out of the sense-making.

David Rock and Jeffrey Schwarz observe that 'for insights to be useful, they need to be generated from within, not given to individuals as conclusions.'[10] 'Like an egg, if it's broken from the outside by others, life doesn't survive, but if it's broken from within, life starts,' add management consultants Colin Price and Sharon Toye.[11]

The role of the coach is to stay in partnership and bear witness as the thinker's insights emerge in the same way that a chick emerges from an eggshell.

When you break the egg for them, you have broken partnership. You can't make meaning for them. Your role is not to force it, but to notice when it happens. This takes humility, courage and silence – duct tape, if necessary, to stop making even a sound if you think you can see meaning emerging.

TRY THIS WITH A PEER COACH

To help the thinker make meaning:
- Play back a single significant word you heard and add a question mark at the end: *Success?* – then wait.
- Invite the thinker to complete an unfinished sentence like, *and success for you is...*
- Simply ask *So?*

---

[9] Weick, Sutcliffe & Obstfeld (2005)

[10] Rock & Schwarz (2006)

[11] Price & Toye (2017)

STAYING IN SYNC

Deep listening and great questions are acknowledged as fundamental building blocks of coaching by all professional bodies but even the most skilled listener and question-asker can lose connection with the thinker. Partnership is broken. You don't need to wait for post-session reflection to find you were out of sync. You can get feedback live in the room from the thinker by checking in. This gives you both useful information to recalibrate what is happening here and now in the conversation. Perhaps the thinker made a leap forward in the silence and now you are out of sync. Or you may be following a hunch. Unless you check in and renegotiate what you need to do now, you are not sharing responsibility for the conversation. You can lose connection with each other and they will start to follow you.

Forgetting to check in, being afraid to ask or loving going off piste are all leading. None of them demonstrate partnership or humility! You may have a great question or technique that feels like a tangent. You may have been engaged to offer hybrid coaching with an expectation of sharing wisdom or information. You are deciding what to do unless you check in by asking permission: *Is this useful?*, **before** they feel obliged to follow you.

THE MOMENT

The way you work together in a conversation and the questions that you ask build up to a moment where the thinker gets an insight and transformation happens. There is no way to predict or control when that will be. There will be times where it takes a couple of sessions for that moment to come. Claire saw it happen in a session three minutes into the work.

What's the least you need to do together for them to feel seen and heard and get to that moment? Over time you hope that there will be other moments. For now, your role is to keep the thinker in flow as you move together into exploring areas that are useful for them and take them into new insight. You won't know how to do that unless you ask. Often. Partnership is what is important here. Your questions only need to be good enough to be useful. And you only know that if you check in.

Checking in, gently and often, is the only way to stay in partnership. When you lead, they follow. Checking in makes the conversation more effective for the thinker and makes the work easier for you!

HOW TO CHECK IN

You'll find your own way – just keep it forward facing. That means avoiding u-turns that might sound like *When we started we said you wanted to do 'this'. Has anything we have done so far at all addressed that?* You had been facing the future and now you have turned round and gone back to the beginning of the conversation. The thinker may well say yes to avoid upsetting you. That's why you need to check in early and often. Avoid any questions that suggest: *Is this working?* or *Am I being any good today?*

TRY THIS

- *How are we doing?*
- *Are we on track?*
- *What insights have you had so far? We use this one very early on before we even think they may have had some. It focuses the conversation and reminds us both that we are here to get some!*
- *Is this useful?*
- *What do you know now that you didn't know when we started?*
- *Where are we now?*
- *What do we need to do now?*
- *We have 20 (or five) minutes left, what's the most important thing we need to do between now and the end?*

WHEN TO CHECK IN

- In an hour, we probably check in 15 or more times. Not so much that it irritates them – and with as few words as possible.
- Before you expect them to have had any insights – it's a great way of normalizing that you are working out how to do this together.
- Before you panic that you don't know what to do.
- Every time you see that the thinker has moved in their thinking (words or body). This is because there may have been some internal movement or insight as well, so you need to keep in sync – you, the thinker and their internal dialogue.
- When they come back after a long silence and deep thinking.
- When there's an energy dip or change of breathing: Claire was watching a recording with coach Natalie Marguet. There was something dissonant about the thinker's breathing. *Her breathing didn't come with her,* noticed Natalie. The best thing about working in partnership is that you have no need to affix meaning to that. All you need to do is notice and offer: *I notice you've stopped breathing?*
- It's common for the thinker to change their tone when they get an insight, so listening for that is a useful check in.
- When you're half-way through.
- When there's been a change of direction away from what you agreed you were doing.
- When you come to a crossroads and before you decide where to go.

WHO LEADS AND WHO FOLLOWS

Lucia recalls when her kids were younger:

They used to play a trust game with my husband. They would put on a blindfold so that they couldn't see and then let their dad guide them on a walk. They would ask him where they had to go and trusted that he would not let them crash into a tree.

When you are working in partnership, and feel comfortable not knowing, you are demonstrating this same level of trust and partnership with the thinker. You are blind. You don't know what is going on in their mind, what is important to explore, what they are experiencing, what is difficult for them, where they are heading in the conversation. You trust them and ask. They lead. You follow. They understand that this is their conversation and that you will shape it together. This is their world, their life, their choice, their work. You are simply keeping them company as they do the work.[12]

When there is not enough partnership, the coach is leading and the thinker is following. We hear a lack of flow. There is a disconnection between the answer and the following question. Flow comes when the question emerges from or connects to the previous answer.

LOOK FOR THIS

In your last coaching session, think about where you may have:
- led intentionally or unintentionally;
- followed or not followed.

Now ask yourself: *What was the impact on the thinker?*

TRANSITIONAL MOMENTS AND BEING COMFORTABLE NOT KNOWING

The greatest potential for partnership in coaching, and the greatest risk of it being broken, are at the transition moments when you're

---

[12] Pedrick (2020)

moving from one question, or indeed silence, to another, and in the space between the answer and the next question. We will talk more about what this looks and sounds like in the next few chapters. For now, it's enough to recognize that how much control you take in those transitional moments, when you don't know what to do next, will shape partnership. When you are driven by the urge to ask a question, your body and facial expressions demonstrate that you want to jump into the conversation. This can interrupt the thinker's thinking.

Even when you are silent, you are communicating something. Moderating your approach every time there is a moment of transition is crucial to keep the flow of the conversation so that you stay in connection. You may need to wait longer than you normally do in other conversations. Becoming more comfortable with silence means waiting until they are ready for you and accepting that there are many details you will never know. You simply need to open up space for their thinking with no need to worry about formulating the next question.

Partnership is not about you. It is about working together so that they become better individuals and transform their lives as they want to. Doing the work together builds the trust you need for deeper work more quickly than anything else. You are saying that you believe they can solve their own problems. Partnership is an art that connects you.

WHEN PARTNERSHIP IS NOT ENOUGH

Coaching credentials are awarded on training, experience, written assessments or by observing recordings of what the coach does in the conversation. What matters most is the impact that the work does or does not have on the thinker. An excellent transcript will be mismatched by a lack of partnership in the conversation when someone is *doing coaching.* Artful coaching isn't about what the coach does. It is about what it evokes in the thinker and in the *space between.*[13] That requires

---

[13] Hawkins & Turner (2019)

the thinker and the coach to be in flow. If you have a list of questions you like to use, use them with care. We don't have any!

You can't have too much partnership. When the thinker responds to a series of questions with *I don't know,* you asking *And if you did know?* is a great partnership question unless they really don't know. Then the thinker feels one down. In recordings you'll hear freezing. How can you partner the next steps of the dance if they don't know what to do? Inviting the thinker to introduce a metaphor about what they are experiencing – mud, quicksand, etc – is one way that might help both of you to navigate something that is difficult to explain so that you can work out together how you move forward.

Even when partnership is strong, you will hear a lot of *I don't know.* When you give space, or negotiate a change of direction for now, this can be followed by the thinker deepening their thinking. They think they don't know and your silence gives them permission to go deeper to find the answer.

When you co-create the conversation about the thinker and what is in their gift – what they can influence – you are in partnership. Now they know that they have to do the work. This is where transformation can happen.

Between us, we have facilitated nearly 20,000 hours of coaching conversations and spent hundreds of hours mastering the technical aspects of coaching. We don't know how to coach anyone unless we co-create the conversation together. You cannot work in partnership when:

- you are doing more thinking than the thinker;
- you lead and they follow;
- you accidentally decide what to do;
- you assume you are on track without asking them.

> **THINK ABOUT**
>
> - What are your strategies to stay more in partnership going forward?
> - What are the pitfalls?
> - Which quality from Part I will enable you to move more into partnership?

In coaching, two (or more) people come together in partnership physically or virtually as the coach facilitates a space for the thinker to think, feel and process. Technical competence only gets you so far in knowing how to listen and what to ask. Artful coaching emerges out of the human-to-human partnership: how close or far away you are, how you share the space, the time and the work. This presence can be seen, heard and sensed through words, sounds and movement.

CHAPTER 8
THE DANCE

Partnership in coaching is often described using the metaphor 'dancing in the moment'. The dance of coaching is the flow of the conversation, which we explore throughout this book. It also embraces the way we physically move in the conversation. Embodied cognition shows us that we think with our whole body, not just the mind.[1] Moving matters. Whether it is a real dance, or simply walking, embodied cognition explains that 'movement is thinking'.[2]

The interaction between the two of you is about what you each see and sense in the other as well as what you hear or say. You see physical movements: speaking, breathing, gestures. This is the movement of coaching. So is having the courage to use physical movement.

Let's look at different aspects of the dance to explore the impact they can have in coaching when you have the courage to use physical movement.

PARTNERSHIP IN THE MOMENT

Dancers Trevor Copp and Jeff Fox presented a TED talk (and dancing demo) about liquid leadership: 'What if a couple could lead and follow each other and switch and switch back – what if it could be like a conversation taking it in turns speaking and listening?'[3] In

---

[1] Shapiro & Spaulding (2021)

[2] Kim Witten in conversation with 3D Coaching.

[3] Copp & Fox, *Liquid Lead Dancing.*

dance, the man has traditionally been the lead and the woman has followed. In liquid leading, dancers move seamlessly between who is leading and who is following. They describe the transitional step as being the core skill of partnership.

In dance, transitional steps happen in the micro moments between two different steps. These moments work best when they are co-created and when both partners agree to the transition through a look, an offer, a silence, a pause, a feeling. Despite changing from one thing to the next, the dancers stay in connection with each other. They will stumble when one of them tries to lead the other into something else without agreement and permission.

You can stumble in coaching when the thinker is silently in flow and you change the subject by asking a question that you have been holding for a while. They stop, answer it and ask, *Was that the answer you were looking for?* You broke their flow by changing the subject when you couldn't hold the silence any longer. Leading with consent might look like *Are you ready for a question?* Gain consent by asking a question followed by *if that's useful?*. The work of coaching happens in the silence, in the words and the movement. Unless you lead with consent, you are choosing when to move on and what to do next. Partnership means that you choose together.

Full partnership has limits. Coach and linguist Kim Witten says:

Taking up space in any form, whether with our words or with our bodies, is an act of being which necessarily impinges on others. This can be more or less intrusive, depending on the context, the relationship and other factors.

The degree of imposition varies. Statements do this more than questions, gestures do this more than stillness, interruptions do this more than silence. But this is key because it relates to everything, from privilege to partnership and beyond. We as humans take up space. And we must be cognizant of the space we inherently take up, especially within the coaching container, which is like a beautiful dance floor we move upon. We must find the balance between taking up enough space to be our expressive and authentic selves (with our words and movements) while being conscious of not overstepping boundaries, causing stumbles (verbal or otherwise), or crowding and imposing onto others.[4]

Transitions in the coaching partnership come from the offers, observations, silence, and the waiting when a small piece of your work is complete and you move into working out together what to do next. When you check in and lightly negotiate what happens next together, you are getting to the heart of partnership. You need to stay in connection or you will stumble when you try to lead the other into something else without agreement or permission. They can lead without permission. It's their conversation. Their dance. Great coaching requires enormous trust in the partnership particularly when you get into more difficult areas.

Claire has watched hundreds of hours of the UK TV programme *Strictly Come Dancing* (and its US counterpart *Dancing with the Stars*) and knows a bit about what makes great dancing. But she doesn't know how to dance. We cannot learn the art of dancing or coaching from a book alone. We learn by doing it.

To an outsider, the Argentine Tango may look weird. Tango is a seamless sequence of turns, stops, sweeps, falls and glides – of leading and following. It is an improvisation that develops on the dance floor. Coaching is also an improvisation that can look weird to an outsider! Like dancing, skilled coaching involves the coach being fully responsive to the movement of the thinker, always allowing them to choose what happens next. We 'lead and follow each other and switch and switch back,' describe Trevor and Jeff.[5]

---

[4] Kim Witten in conversation with 3D Coaching.

[5] Copp & Fox, *Liquid Lead Dancing*.

Josephine Knowles is a coach and a teacher of Argentine Tango. She came to *The Coaching Inn* podcast to talk about the connections between dancing and coaching:

> Every single moment is an improvised moment. You're sharing a physical space together. If one is too overpowering, the other person is leaning back. You have to find your middle ground and hold the space together. What I love about tango is that you have to connect to the heart first. You're connecting with your chest, and it almost doesn't matter what the steps are.
>
> I've heard coaches who reel out… models. They're important and if the connection (partnership) isn't there it really doesn't work.
>
> The best tango for me is that you don't really know who's leading and who's following… You are fully present to the moment and you're fully present to the process… You are actually in your body rather than in your head thinking where do I need to take them? And what goals do they need to do?
>
> I don't want to be in my head thinking. In coaching, how do I move into my body so that my body is giving me data, giving me an idea of maybe where they're coming from, where there's tension maybe, or where there's lack of breath. That's what I do in tango.[6]

In coaching, staying in partnership looks simple, but can be one of the hardest things to learn. Josephine starts by teaching aspiring tango dancers to walk:

---

[6] Knowles (2021)

Walking is the hardest thing to do in tango because it involves every single element. So we focus a lot on walking. You need your balance. You need your core. You need your head in the right place. You need your heart in the right place. And you need to be able to walk on the beat. And if you're not sharing that all together, it can go really wrong.[7]

Your capacity or willingness to work in partnership will connect back to what brought you to coaching in the first place. Coaching is about facilitating someone else to do good work. When your deepest desire is to help, partnership becomes trickier. Kathryn Mannix says that 'rather than enabling, over-helping builds dependence: they dance on our shoes as we make the steps, but they don't learn the steps for themselves.'[8] At first sight that might look like partnership, but when the thinker dances on your shoes, they are following you.

WHAT IS SEEN

Josephine describes feeling dominated: 'I've danced with amazing dancers where I felt like a complete beginner. They pull you around and you end up feeling exhausted and sweaty.'[9] In coaching, that might look like you are leading the direction, even when the questions are not useful. It may be about being too far apart, too close together, or you take the lead because the thinker is unsure about where to go next and they feel they will demonstrate weakness if they say that. Watching recordings is the only way to see what is happening and notice the dance.

Coach and academic Tünde Erdös explored partnership and presence through her research into the power of the non-verbal

---

[7] Ibid

[8] Mannix (2021)

[9] Knowles (2021)

relationship.[10] [11] She looked at movement through video-only recordings of coaching sessions, which analysed motion energy, spontaneous movement and how the coach and client responded to each other non-verbally. Over ten sessions were recorded with each coach/client pair. Neither knew what was being analysed. Three data sets were collected: the video evidence, exit interviews with coaches about how they evaluated each session, and exit interviews with the client about how they were feeling. When the video analysis showed incongruence and a mismatch of energies between the coach and client, the coach would report that the session felt great. How thinkers and coaches experience the dance of coaching can be very different.

USING MOVEMENT

We believe that physical movement plays an important role in the dance between the coach and the thinker. Without becoming totally self-conscious, notice a little about how what is seen impacts the conversation. We don't endorse the use of body language analysis because that becomes very diagnostic.

LOOK FOR THIS

Watch a video recording of coaching with the sound off.
- Notice when the thinker moves. What do you see?
- Check their facial expressions. Are they changing as they talk?
- Watch how they breathe. Are they breathing, or even holding their breath?
- Consider how you can use movement as a question in response to what you see and sense.

---

[10] Erdös (2021b)

[11] Erdös (2021a)

HOW WE MOVE

What is your body saying about whether you are leading or following? When you lean in, it can be received as an interruption. When you are too still for too long, they might feel you want them to tell you more of their story. Notice how they respond to your leaning in or to long periods of stillness. If they recognize a cue and perceive it as a signal to wrap up their turn, they may stumble in their speech, or consciously or unconsciously receive the message that you are about to speak.

QUESTIONS TO THINK ABOUT

- How does your movement make you bigger or smaller than the thinker?
- Online, where are you in the frame of the picture?
- How is your position or movement facilitating or impeding the creative space for the thinker?

HOW YOU MOVE TOGETHER

The dance of coaching can be seen in the way you move together. Growing coaches focus on what to say or ask and how to listen well. The way you move can help the thinker shift perspective and get unstuck. It can also accidentally keep them stuck. Online, with people who work remotely, you may find yourself coaching someone who has sat at the same screen in the same chair for several years. If that is the chair where they got stuck, where they have talked about this thing with other people, and thought about it a lot, coaching at the same screen in the same chair and talking about it again will not easily get them unstuck.

It takes courage to ask, *Shall we move?* when they say *I have been stuck for weeks.* Always ask permission, and never ask them to do something you're not willing or able to do yourself at the same time. There is nothing more unequal than inviting someone to stand while you are sitting down. When you move together you are making it safe and less awkward.

After a coaching demo, people will ask us *Why did you ask them to stand?* It is always because the thinker told us to. Notice the words they use that invite movement: *If only I could stand back and see it differently, I need a next step.* These can elicit an invitation from you: *Shall we stand and take one?*

How are you using movement to co-create the dance? What is the role of stillness, and not moving, in your conversations? Be still when they are speaking and thinking. You want to create space and to not interfere with their flow.

The only limit to using movement is your courage and the willingness of how far this particular thinker is willing to go.

YOUR FACE

Dancers use different facial expressions to evoke emotion and enable the audience to experience different phases of a dance. How you use your face impacts how the thinker progresses through the conversation. Pay attention to the sounds you make to say, *I hear you, Keep talking* and *Was that an insight?* And make sure that your face is giving the same message.

Watching back videos is the only way to notice the impact of your expressions. Your furrowed brow may be an expression of listening deeply. It may be perceived as judgement or confusion or be received as an invitation for them to explain more to you. And if you are frowning when they have an insight, they may not notice that the insight has come.

TRANSITION AND CONNECTION

Recordings show that the flow is broken when the questions from the coach are disconnected from what the thinker has just shared: the coach is not responding to what's unfolding in front of them.

You might see that the coach is not looking at the thinker. They may even be looking at their notes. When the thinker returns from their thinking, they are out of sync. They do not get back in sync because the coach is not checking in at moments of transition. They are dancing on their own and pulling the thinker into their own dance. The thinker has little power and is now following the coach's dance. They have lost connection. They are in different thinking processes and the conversation is unlikely to be transformational.

When we watch videos where the coach reports that something was 'off' in the session, the most likely reason is that they weren't looking. They missed a transitional moment where the thinker received the beginning of a question and was ready to dance. Instead of going deeper, the thinker waited for the coach to finish talking. It is only by watching the thinker that you can stay in sync.

LOOK FOR THIS

Watch a video recording of your own coaching.
- Notice your facial expressions. What do they communicate during a coaching conversation?
- Think about how your facial expression might communicate these things:
  - I am with you.
  - Was that an insight?
  - I have something important to say.
  - This question is an offer.

Dance partners check in intuitively when the dance seems to be changing, when they are out of step, or to learn whether they both want to continue this dance. These are all cues to signal transition. In music, the cue is usually a sound – or an absence of sound. In coaching, you see and hear the transitional moments if you're looking. All these transitions require both partners to adapt their distance – sometimes closer, sometimes far away. In coaching, you pay enough attention to notice the signs of a transition even when your inner voice has a beautiful question lined up. This takes courage and humility to believe that you will work out what to do together.

CHAPTER 9
THE WORDS

We are laughing in the Dolomites as we struggle to find the right words to write about words! In a coaching conversation, words are easy to find because *we* don't need to find them, *thinkers* do.

The words we hear are part of the coaching encounter. They are the lyrics to the music we are co-creating. How we respond to the thinker's words depends on how they are communicating them and how we are receiving them. A coaching app on a phone can use the same words as we do. The additional human qualities that bring depth, connection and flow to the conversation include how we move as we each speak, the sound of our words and our silences, and the level of trust that we sense between us. What can we learn about the way we use words that will make the coaching more useful?

TRY THIS

If you want an insight into how you actually use words, a written transcript will record exactly what was said and for how long. You will see areas where you are engaging well, and you can see things to develop. A transcript comes as quite a shock if you discover that you are talking more often or for longer than you thought. And it is useful. You are not paid by the number of words you say. You are paid to facilitate the thinking of another person.[1]

THEIR WORDS

We encounter people who use words in many ways: lots of words or just a few, complex words or jargon. Some people lack confidence in using the right words. Some might be speaking to us in a second or third language. Others might enjoy silence more than words. Words are only a part of what we hear. The intonation, pace and the energy in someone's voice adds to the music and shapes the way they communicate.

People moderate words all the time. As you start to work together, you will subconsciously notice their style and adapt to it. The language you use to talk to a fisherman at the market is different from talking to a customer or a politician. You adapt to match the words someone else uses. And you do that to connect, so that you can understand each other better.

Many books and methods teach you to match not only the thinker's communication style but also their words, so that they can feel heard and understood. This is effective. And sometimes you are offering back information that they already know. We offer dissonant words when we want to challenge or spark a new insight:

Thinker: I have been working at the same company for almost a decade, and I've climbed the ladder to become a senior executive. While I'm proud of my accomplishments, I feel like I've hit a ceiling in terms of growth and development. I'm comfortable in my role, but I know that I need something new and challenging to reignite my passion for what I do.

Coach: Stuck? Change?

Thinker: Yes! Change is exactly what I need but I'm not stuck. I've begun to explore different options and considered various industries, trying to find the right fit for me. I'm thinking of becoming an entrepreneur and starting my own business.

The coach has an intuition about the need for change and offers it lightly, with a question mark, to invite further exploration. The coach offers the words *stuck* and *change*. The thinker decides what is useful.

SUMMARIZING

Listening to the thinker's story can feel like receiving an enormous download of information. It can be overwhelming if you don't keep the right distance. Just like Marco's canvas, if you are too close, you will get lost. Claire talks about capturing the *headlines* by offering back a sense of the theme that is being communicated in the story, and the *underbelly* to indicate the emotion that emerges in the space between you.[1] Marilyn Franklin describes this as having a *helicopter view*.[2]

We hear coaches offer back information that the thinker already knows. People know facts. Offering them back does not give them new insight and may slow down the flow. You can instead offer something new, inviting a deeper exploration and responding to the thinker by building on what they say as an offer:

Coach: Becoming an entrepreneur? And how does that feel?

It takes practice to know when to offer the same words they use, and when to offer something different. You won't always get it right.

EMPHASIS

When you are listening, you might wonder whether some words might be more significant or bigger than others, even when the thinker maintains the same tone as they talk. The words might feel like a bomb exploding in your head, and the thinker might not notice the weight of what they have said: imagine someone describing their

---

[1] Pedrick (2020)
[2] Franklin (2019)

workplace and dropping in lightly, *I don't trust my people* or *I'm not sure I'm worth this financial effort* or *This isn't who I am.* At other times, the significance, or weight, might emerge across disconnected comments. In isolation, none of them feel heavy. Together, a more significant theme might be emerging: *They all know each other / We're not included / I feel different.*

When people are engaged in a conversation and busy putting their thoughts into words, they may not realize they are giving different weight to what they say. You will, when you pay attention. The art is to offer back in exactly the same way you heard them speak and wait for what emerges from their silence. Their answer is likely to be a 'oh yes…' and then they will discover more for themselves. And if there is wisdom in what they said, you need to offer in a way that they own the wisdom as their own:

- This is not who I am?
- Not belonging?

TRY THIS

Watch someone on a documentary or the news on TV. Then try one of the following:
- Summarize the theme of what they are saying using less than five words.
- Notice one or two words that you sense have a different weight.

ANSWER AND QUESTION, NOT QUESTION AND ANSWER

Artful coaching does not come from the flow between the question and the answer. You keep in flow when you transition well from their answer to your next question. In their answer, they are likely to have been moving forward in their thinking. Your next question needs to connect with where they are now, using their words and tone – unless you are making an intentional choice to be dissonant.

Even when using the thinker's words, coaches will often over-explain questions, or ask them twice to offer them in a clearer and better articulated way. When you are forming questions in flow and building from what the thinker has said, remember that they were also there when your question was forming! Your words are in context. There is no need to explain.

INTERRUPTING

Can you interrupt when your role as a coach is to be in a conversation where someone feels heard? Yes you can. You don't need to interrupt when they are venting unless it is to check in whether that's what they want to do as part of the conversation. And you need to interrupt when the thinker is:

- heading backwards into the past;
- stuck in the story;
- oversharing;
- talking a lot because they think you need to know, or just using many words.

The art of interrupting is to do it in a way that is future focused. The only things you can influence in this conversation are the present and the future. When you interrupt in a way that takes the thinker backwards, you can lose connection with them by sounding judgemental. For example, when you have lost track of the focus:

Coach:	When we started, we agreed to explore a plan for that meeting.
Thinker:	(*Thinks: Oh no, I haven't done what my coach wanted – let me try and remember what that was.*)

Your interruption has taken the thinker backwards. Future focused sounds like:

Coach: How are we doing on getting to a plan?

When there are a lot of words, So today? is a great interrupter.

LOOK FOR THIS

Listen to a recording and notice:
- how the coach's questions pick up from the thinker's answer;
- where the coach introduces words that don't resonate with the thinker;
- when the coach's interventions interrupt the flow.

SILENT WORDS

Sometimes there are words that do not need to be spoken. They pause. There is something going on in their head. They might want to share, they might not. You can simply invite exploration. And then they choose. For example: *There is a lot going on in your head, what do we need to think about here?*

OUR WORDS

We have talked about the words the thinker brings. What about you? People become coaches because they are good with words. You don't have to use them all. Talking too much, for too long, or using language the thinker doesn't understand shifts the focus to you. Whatever words you use, make sure they are easy to understand and connect to where you are in the conversation. Questions need to be short, clear and straightforward. You ask a question, not because you need the answer, but so that it will cause them to think. What are the fewest words you can use to move them forward?

Thinker: I've been working at my company for several years, and I love my job. I enjoy working with my co-workers, and we have always got along well. However, over the past few months, tensions have begun to rise within our team and conflicts started to emerge. At first, I thought it was just a temporary blip, and I assumed that the conflicts would resolve themselves over time. But as the conflicts continue, I realize that something needs to be done to address the underlying issues. I've reflected on the situation and tried to identify the root causes of the conflicts. I realize that there are underlying tensions and disagreements that have been building for some time, and that these issues have never been properly addressed.

Coach: What are the underlying causes of the workplace conflict, and what strategies can be implemented to address the root issues and promote a positive and productive work environment for all team members involved?

In this example the coach replies with three questions. Which one should the thinker answer? They won't even remember the first question by the time the coach has finished speaking. And often the first question is the best!

Here are some examples of how artful coaches might respond:

Coach 1: Tensions, conflicts, disagreements. And today?

Coach 2: Quite some turbulence in the last few months! And what question would you like to explore together today?

Coach 3: Underlying tensions for quite some time! And what about this do we need to think about today?

More artful coaches pick on the themes they have just heard and then ask a question that makes the topic the right size for today.

HABITS

What are the habits you know you have with words?

- Phrases that are useful when said once can become distracting and irritating for the thinker when they hear them repeatedly in the same conversation: *I am hearing you saying you're stressed*, try simply offering the headline, *Stress?*
- Stacking questions – see what they do with the first before you ask the second.
- Explaining the meaning of the question or explaining what made you choose the question.
- Repeating *I hear you* many times. When the thinker feels heard, they know you hear them. Save this one for when it really matters.
- Using jargon. You don't need to use the words you read in books you might understand: *What are your limiting beliefs?* They might not understand! Stay simple: *Sounds like something is getting in the way? Holding you back?*
- As long as they want to be there, when you use a lot of words, the thinker will say very little. When you say less, they say more.

You'll find words that work for you – make sure they work for the thinker, too.

UNDERSTANDING

You don't need to understand the meaning of every word they say. And sometimes there are words the thinker uses where it is important for you to have enough of a common understanding. When it comes to words, artful coaching is knowing which words to use and which ones to drop. And that will be different in every single conversation. For example:

Thinker: I want to talk about success.
Coach: What do you mean by success?

At the beginning of a conversation, asking for clarity on meaning will result in you understanding more without them getting any new insight. You don't need to know the meaning at this stage.

Here is an example when you both need to understand the meaning and they need to clarify it for themselves.

Thinker: By the end of this conversation I'll know how to achieve success in that meeting.
Coach: Success?
Thinker: [*goes on to explain more*]

When they use a word to describe the outcome of the conversation, you both need to understand where you are going.

QUESTIONS TO THINK ABOUT

- What are your strategies to use words better going forward?
- What could be challenging for you?
- What needs to shift in you to improve the way you use words?

Words are a significant part of the art of coaching. The best questions come from the thinker, so mostly using their words can improve partnership and flow and build towards transformation.

What your words sound like – your pace, your tone and your timing – are as important as what they mean.

CHAPTER 10
THE MUSIC

The music of coaching is the sound of the conversation. When you bring the words, the movement and the sound together, you co-create a unique performance each and every time you meet for coaching. Song lyrics often need to be paired with the sound of the music to make sense. In the same way, the words in coaching transcripts need to be heard within the broader context of the conversation to be fully understood.

You might remember reading the lyrics on an album sleeve. Imagine reading the lyrics of Queen's 'Bohemian Rhapsody' without the music: 'Galileo Figaro, magnifico.'[1] You get a clearer sense of what is actually being communicated when you hear the words and the music together. This is why it's possible to read a transcript of a coaching session where the words you see are technically perfect – and then discover from the recording that the sound is clunky and dissonant.

You can listen to the sound of a conversation without the words. Listening to recordings in other languages has been a rich learning lab that is deepening our understanding of the musicality of the conversation when we don't understand the words.

PARTNERSHIP IN THE SOUND AND THE WORDS

What is in the sound of the conversation that demonstrates partnership? 'When a coach is comfortable using a range of modes

---

[1] Queen, 'Bohemian Rhapsody', written by Freddie Mercury, released as a single (1975).

and orchestrates the dialogue to become rich "music" of high and low, rich and light notes, we are seeing mastery at work,' says coach Hetty Einzig.[2] The only way that you can really know if that's happening is by watching recordings where you can notice the sound of the tune, tone, rhythm, timing and silence that make the words come alive. You can see the impact of how you do what you do on your partner in the conversation. You can listen to the music and watch the dance. This is where you can see the human side of coaching.

In partnership, the sound and the words are equally important. Silence and humility are demonstrated through the sound of your questions, your tone and timing. The same question can be experienced as a statement or an offer depending on how it sounds. When partnership is strong, you can hear the energy that emerges as someone is gaining new insight. As you work, the flow brings you together. It is co-created when you are working in harmony.

You can hear when a conversation is not in flow. You might bring eloquently sounding and beautifully formed questions but you are not in partnership when they are waiting for you to finish talking. When the sound of the thinker's voice is fluent, like reading a story book, they may be telling you things they know already. Their thinking might not be in flow.

The sound of thinking is often disfluent. When they are in flow and working things out as they are talking, they will pause to notice things in new ways. As they bring together different thoughts and feelings, the sound will change. This is the sound of insight. When it is your turn to speak, picking up that sound will keep you in flow.

You won't necessarily get in flow during the first session. The first time thinkers experience being in flow, notice how it supports their thinking and brings them new awareness; you will experience partnership in a new way. There is a deeper connection between you and greater trust in the process. Next time, this is what they will expect and it will be easier to go deeper.

---

[2] Einzig (2017)

Video recordings help you notice when you are in flow together. You can begin to see and hear when you have broken flow by changing the music, broken the silence too early or when your need to control is keeping the conversation transactional. Not all breaking of silence is bad. Sometimes you break silence to make different music together.

Listening to the flow of sounds and words is where you can learn more about how to co-create the partnership. This is fundamental to growing the trust and presence required to do good and deep work.

SIGN THAT CONVERSATIONS ARE OUT OF FLOW

- At the beginning, the rightsizing questions sound disconnected from what the thinker is saying. The coach takes a breath: *What do we need to focus on today?* It sounds like the coach didn't hear what the thinker said.
- In the middle, the thinker may be going around in circles, you both seem to be stuck and the coach doesn't speak.
- Towards the end:
  - The coach and the thinker are surprised that the conversation is over and they are talking about something that they agree is too big to explore during the remainder of the session.
  - The coach is hesitant about wrapping up because they doubt the thinker made any progress at all and asks questions that indicate this: *Did you make any progress today?*

SIGNS THAT CONVERSATIONS ARE IN FLOW

- At the beginning, the rightsizing questions connect to what the thinker is saying: *Stress?; Overwhelm?; Strategies?; Which bit of that do we need to focus on?*
- In the middle, both the coach and the thinker are able to seamlessly navigate the uncertainty: *Where shall we take this conversation next?*

- Towards the end, the thinker is not surprised that the conversation is over because the coach and the thinker have been co-creating the end together: *What do we need to do in the five minutes we have left?*

WHOSE TUNE IS IT?

You will have preferences about how you work. If every session you deliver with different people looks and sounds the same, it is unlikely that you are making the most of co-creating the work together. This is improvising music, like jazz, and always playing the same tune.

Claire co-created a conversation with a thinker in a coaching demo. In the debrief, one of the group said, *I didn't know you were a somatic coach*. The coaching was somatic because the thinker spoke entirely about what they were experiencing in their body. Someone else said, *I wouldn't have liked it if you had coached me like that*. The thinker decided how to work and Claire followed. A different session with a different person would have sounded different. Great coaching emerges when you improvise together in the moment. Their work. Their tune.

If you have just learned a new tool or technique and would like to try it out with someone, remember that it needs to flow with the work that they want to do. Be careful of imposing your preferences (your favourite tune) in someone else's conversation. For example, if you have just been on Gestalt training, you might want to do an empty chair exercise in your next conversation. The risk is that you are listening to see how to fit it in rather than listening to the thinker.

LISTEN TO THE SOUND

The sound of your words influences the partnership. This is where the human coach differs from the bot. Tone is 'a quality in the voice that expresses the speaker's feelings or thoughts, often towards the person being spoken to.'[3] Tone brings useful data into the coaching conversation. Notice the tone, pace and pitch as the thinker is processing. Notice when they go outside their normal range. That might be an indicator that something has changed. Listen for tone as much as you listen to the words. Remember that information they share is stuff they already know. The tone and the way they say things shows where it is new information for them.

Your tone, pace and pitch are unique. In English, the tone or pace will change a little when someone gets an insight. For example, while they are stuck you might hear a flat or monotone where the words they are saying all have a similar sound. When they have an insight, the tone might change.

In Communication Accommodation Theory, *convergence* (resonance) happens when you deliberately or naturally match 'pronunciation, pause and utterance lengths, vocal intensities, non-verbal behaviours, and intimacy of self-disclosures.'[4] [5] In coaching, this builds trust. It's comfortable. Matching the rhythms, sounds and words creates a closeness between you without having to be explicit. You are in flow. Now the deeper work can begin.

Divergence (dissonance) happens when you are deliberately or naturally being different from the thinker. In Communication Accommodation Theory this can be seen as power play. In coaching, you can dissonate when you want to challenge or disrupt flow. This creates distance, and when used wisely, can trigger change. You might use a different tone when you want to calm someone down who is agitated and seems angry: lowering volume and slowing down the pace of the conversation can de-escalate the emotion.

In coaching, dissonance might sound like interrupting, changing the tone or pace, or even moving position. Inviting both of you to stand up, for example, is dissonant. Use dissonance with care. If you are dissonant for too long, you have lost the benefit of the

---

3 Cambridge Dictionary definition. Available from: https://dictionary.cambridge. org/dictionary/english/tone. Accessed August 2023.
4 Giles, Coupland & Coupland (1991)
5 Infante, Rancer & Avtgis (2009)

disruption and have changed the direction of the conversation. You are now playing your tune.

Every coaching conversation is unique. In the commentary of a 2022 BBC Prom Concert, music journalist Tom Service says, 'all we ever have, all of us, is the present tense of this performance.'

LOOK FOR THIS

In a recording, notice how tone changes, and reflect on the following questions:
- Where are the voices of the coach and thinker resonant?
- Where are they dissonant?
- What is the impact of your tone on the thinker?

OFFERING

Make an offer is an improv principle. Claire started hosting presence workshops with coach Stuart Reid after he made an offer saying, *Coaching feels a bit like improv.* Every workshop they learn something new about coaching. Not only is improv a great way to learn to make an offer, but it also builds courage to step in and say what you see even when you don't know what you will say after that.

Author Malcolm Gladwell says that 'bad improvisers block action, often with a high degree of skill. Good improvisers develop action.'[6] The way you ask a question can close things down or open things up. Statements block thinking – with a high degree of skill. Offers develop exploration and lead to action. Asking a question with a statement tone stops conversations flowing. It sounds like tell. The thinker will wait for the next question, or ask, *Is that the answer you were looking for?* Great coaching is about doing the least you need to do for the thinker to get in flow. That takes humility and humanity.

---

[6] Gladwell (2005)

WHAT DOES AN OFFER SOUND LIKE?

Intonation is 'the sound changes produced by the rise and fall of the voice when speaking, especially when this has an effect on the meaning of what is said.'[7] Intonation is used to add more information about the intention behind what you are saying.

Questions need to sound like an offer so that they are heard as an invitation: *You're tired*↗*?* (with rising intonation).

You're tired↘*?* (with falling intonation) looks like a question but sounds like a statement. It feels like someone is diagnosing or telling you that you are tired.

You can move position at the same time as using a change in tone that offers *I think you may have more to say here? Go deeper?* This offer is heard and seen.

If you are building your coaching hours by working with other coaches, you may find that they answer statements like *You're tired*↘*?* as if they were questions. You can't easily refine how to ask better questions when the thinker is a coach. The more coaches coach coaches who know the words, the sound and the dance of the work, the more you can get stuck in asking questions in a certain way. Coaches are great at being coached.

Thinkers who are not coaches will lose the flow of the conversation because they think you made a statement.

'We offer, and they choose,' says Kathryn Mannix.[8] Partnership is deepened when we make an offer that sounds like an offer.

OK

What are your *I-hear-you*, *Keep-talking* or *Go-on-then* sounds? Are you a lover of OK? Sometimes OK is a soft rhythm, a signal to the thinker that you are in flow together. Sometimes it is a gentle challenge. Sometimes a question. In a video blog, Lucia shared that

---

[7] Cambridge Dictionary definition. Available from: https://dictionary.cambridge.org/dictionary/english/intonation. Accessed August 2023.
[8] Mannix (2021)

the intention of OK might be *I hear you* and it can be heard as 'hurry up' or 'give me more information', 'listen to me' or 'I'm not listening'. O-↘K can be heard as 'wait a second, I'm going to speak.'[9] So they do. It doesn't sound like an offer.

Nancy Kline is very direct: 'Oh, you may think, I'll just grab this tiny pause here to say a little something… and remind them that I'm still here… Forget it. You will kill all that was about to form. You might as well not have started.'[10] 'Mmm' and 'Uh huh' have a similar impact when they are used as *let-me-just-take-that-in-and-think-about-it-for-a-moment* sounds. What sounds or subtle gestures do you have that will sound like an offer and be heard as 'over to you'?

When sounds are unclear, you might be unintentionally communicating something. For example, when they hear from you what they perceive to be a 'listen to me' sound, they will stop thinking.

Unless you indicate that you're passing the conversation back to the thinker, they won't know when you're going to stop talking and they will wait for you. You have accidentally told them that what you want to say is more important than anything they were thinking, even when your contribution is not useful. Your sounds or silence need to keep them in flow.

QUESTIONS TO THINK ABOUT

Listen to a recording of a conversation where you are coaching and notice what your OK does to the thinker.
- How many are you asking?
- How do they impact flow?
- What would be different if you did not ask them?

---

[9] Baldelli's YouTube channel, Coaching Outside the Box. Available from: https://youtu.be/KerM7ae7PHU. Accessed August 2023.

[10] Kline (2020)

TONE AS CHALLENGE

Tone can be used in different ways. Keeping tone the same can sound like:

Thinker: [*steady tone*] I pro-ba-bly know what to do.
Coach: Uh huh [*match tone*]
Thinker: [*stays stuck (monotone) for a few more minutes because they didn't hear themselves*]

Watching recordings, we often observe the thinker having an insight which neither they nor the coach have noticed. Changing tone can enable the thinker to recognize an insight:

Thinker: [*steady tone*] I pro-ba-bly know what to do.
Coach: Ah [mismatch *higher tone*]
Thinker: Oh yes, I do know! [*tone changes*]

You can use tone in combination with deep listening to notice and lightly offer that perhaps that was an insight. Having a *was-that-an-insight?* sound is useful dissonance that can evoke awareness. We have listened to hundreds of recordings where the coach noticed that the insight had come. When they used their *I-hear-you* tone, the thinker did not realize they had, in fact, moved forward.

QUESTIONS TO THINK ABOUT

- What does your tone communicate during a coaching conversation?
- What are the sounds you use that distinguish:
    - I am with you.
    - Was that an insight?
    - Go on then, keep talking.
    - I have something important to say.
    - This question is an offer.
    - I am telling you something here.

TONE FOR ENDINGS

In music, 'a universally satisfying ending provides clues in the music, through chord progressions, that tell the listener the end of the song is near.'[11] The better you are at creating a safe place to work, the more surprised the thinker will be when it ends. If your work is to be in partnership, you will need to co-create the end. This is another form of checking in, or checking out. It starts from the middle of the conversation: *We have about half an hour left – what do we need to do now?*

We notice that the thinker's tone will change when they have genuinely got a final insight. For example, when you ask, *Is that a good place to finish today?*, the thinker responds in one of three ways. A loud *YES!!* means what it says. So does *No*. The other way is *Ye-a-s*. A hesitant 'yes' always means 'no'. There are many ways to manage this. Simply ask, *What do we need to do in the final couple of minutes so that we have finished?* Claire pays more attention to the sound than to the words when she is coming to the end of a conversation. When you hear the sound change, it is usually accompanied by a facial move. The words, the sound and the movement are in sync. Something has changed.

QUESTIONS TO THINK ABOUT

Think about the last few coaching conversations you've had.
- Where have you noticed the sound and the words working together?
- Where have you noticed a dissonance?

BREATHE

Actor John Wayne used to take a breath mid-sentence to avoid interruption by journalists: 'When challenged as to why he took

---

[11] Pilhofer & Day (2019)

breaths in this way while he spoke, he is reputed to have said, slowly, of course: "Just to let them know... [deep breath]... I ain't done yet.'"[12] You might hold your breath in order to finish asking what feels like a very important question. Your role is actually to let people interrupt you all the time – if it will enable them to move forward with their thinking. You don't need to complete a sentence when the first few words were enough for the thinker to pick up and move their own thinking forward.

How you breathe is received like punctuation: *Here is the first half of my sentence* [breathe] *and wait for me because I still have more to say.* They will wait, and by the time you stop talking it is likely that they will have lost their flow. Conversely, offering the first half of a sentence and inviting them to finish it is artful! *And our question right now is...?*

Noticing the thinker's breath is information. They might describe an insight or a breakthrough while they are holding their breath. You could search for a great question or simply offer: *You're not breathing?*

TRY THIS

Pick up a small object like a ball. Listen to a recording of a conversation. It could be coaching. It might be a radio or TV interview. Choose one hand to represent the person facilitating the conversation, and the other hand to represent the other person. Take the ball in the hand that represents the person who is holding the conversation right now. Pass it to the other hand when the conversation is properly passed over. You can do this several times and notice:

- Who is doing the work?
- Who is holding the power?

---

[12] Eggert (2010)

> - What is the tone that indicates handing over?
> - Where is there a battle, or indeed defeat, in the movement between them?

SILENCE IS COACHING TOO

Without silence, music would lose its variety and emotion. Using silence for a few beats or for a longer time creates very different impacts.

In Chapter 1, we explored the importance of silence inside you so that you can use it in the room. Whether it is through a pause, a breath or a longer silence, the silence that comes from the coach saying nothing can be a significant part of the work of a conversation. Generative silence enables them to do some good work or wonder. This is the place where the thinker is thinking, and your role is to keep them company while they do that. The work is in the silence. Even when the thinker uses a lot of words to work things out for themselves, the deeper work can come when they stop for breath.

WHO DOES THE SILENCE BELONG TO?

The outcome of the conversation belongs to the thinker. It is their life, their future, their resourcefulness. Great coaching isn't about how much noise you make or what you add. It is about you working together and co-creating a composition so that they will continue to play the tune into the future long after you stop working together.

The music, the tone, the silences and the spaces between them are part of the composition. Remember Kathryn Mannix in Chapter 1?

> There are points when nobody is speaking, and the silence is doing the work. Silence is where we ponder, where we bring together different ideas and assemble new possibilities, where we reach new understanding, where we make a

decision or change our minds. In other words, silence is where the real work happens.[13]

In the same way that musical rests can have different impacts, there are all kinds of silence. Make sure that every silence is generated by the thinker, and that they have control of when to come back to the conversation. The only exception is if you go silent to notice what you have heard or seen or sensed. That silence is in service of the thinker. You are looking for something in the space between you.

When you play your own music in your head during the thinker's silence, you are likely to come back in a different key or rhythm that is dissonant from theirs. You will have lost connection.

PACE

In music, staccato creates a clear separation between consecutive notes, almost as if there is a pause between them.[14] Staccato sounds or questions keep the interaction fast. Lucia uses staccato to bring high challenge or when someone is committing to action: *And?... and?... and?*

Without a greater purpose, short questions in quick succession can feel like interrogation leaving little room for silence or processing. You have many great things to ask and the thinker can feel like they are on the other end of an automatic weapon. When the coach is following a script or thinking of a question while the thinker is speaking, questions can come rapidly that sound like statements. Slow down. You will always have enough time when you work in partnership.

Great coaching is so much more than a string of questions. 'Everybody knows that making good music is about more than just stringing a collection of notes together.'[15] Flow comes when you pay

---

[13] Mannix (2021)

[14] Treccani Italian dictionary. Available from: www.treccani.it/vocabolario. Accessed August 2023.

[15] Pilhofer & Day (2019)

attention to timing, pauses and how you respond in words, in sound and in movement. All impact how you are present in the space with the thinker. Is this your pace or theirs?

There's nothing more annoying to a thinker than when the coach's timing is out of sync. Somewhere in your training you will have been on the receiving end of that. Negotiate the timing and pace together, and check in: *Does this pace work for you?*

VOLUME

A musical conductor ensures that the instruments are in tune with each other and that nothing is too loud nor too soft. In conversations, some of what you hear can be overwhelmingly loud and make it difficult to hear the quieter story. What is heard could be dominated by the story of what did and didn't happen. Those are facts. People will remember facts. When they are talking about what happened, who was involved, what they will do, who they will talk to, etc, perhaps you can turn down the volume as you won't need to remember that. When you turn down the volume on information, you can turn it up to notice some of the other parts that might include:

- Emotions.
- Patterns – what's being repeated?
- What's missing?
- The sound of the human?
- The sound of the wider system?

Which line of music do you prefer to listen to? Where do you need to turn up the volume?

Emerging insight in the thinker often comes with a different tempo or volume. They may speed up or slow down and you both get a sense that you are almost there. Your role is to build the music with them. And as they move towards insight, stay silent and let them play their own tune. Leave it with them. This can feel like leaving something hanging and as a human being you can be tempted to be part of the crescendo adding your own meaning as insight emerges. This is the moment to swallow your enthusiasm and watch the great work emerge in the mind, the body and the soul of your thinking companion. Interrupting would be saying you have value to add here. You don't. Celebrate when the insight is beginning to settle. Jumping in too early can sabotage the moment. Charlie Brower suggests: 'A new idea is delicate. It can be killed by a sneer or a yawn; it can be stabbed to death by a quip and worried to death by a frown on the right man's brow.'[16]

WE ALL MAKE MISTAKES

What a relief that there is no such thing as perfect coaching. In jazz,

> Art Tatum once declared, 'There's no such thing as a wrong note.' Wrong notes in jazz are often considered to be opportunities for improvisatory exploration; a note is only wrong if the performer does not know what to do with it.[17]

You're both human. Improvising together is what really matters here. Great coaches ask the wrong questions often. The art is to not make a thing of it and move on. When you apologize it can disrupt the work.

WE MAKE MUSIC TOGETHER

In an hour's coaching conversation, there are usually one or two questions that bring new insight. They cannot be scripted, learned or prepared, and there is no knowing which question will be the unlocker. Coaching is improvisation at its best. Sometimes a run of a few questions will build and the moment of insight will emerge. At other times it won't and you will need to check in and agree what will be useful next. This is out of your control. Leave space, don't

---

[16] Brower, quoted in Maxwell (2003)
[17] Klotz (2017)

break the silence! The right timing is much more important than the right question.

What is the least sound you need to make in service of the thinker feeling seen and heard and having new insights? Even when you're working with the same person over time, every session will sound different. Some sessions will be quite conventional and some will take you both by surprise as you improvise together. You can never repeat the same session twice. They are unique.

Artful coaching is demonstrated when you use models sparingly, adapt them to the situation and the thinker's learning style and make coaching your own. Together.

QUESTIONS TO THINK ABOUT

- What are your strategies to improve the sound of your conversations?
- What could be challenging about this?
- When might you be intentionally dissonant or resonant?

The sound of the conversation conveys more than words. It is from the sound that we establish trust, and they sense who you are. This is where they will experience your vulnerability and humility. They will hear whether you are truly empathic. You may have been using everything we have spoken about here intuitively. Knowing that you know means that now, with courage, you can intentionally use sound to be a catalyst for change.

CHAPTER 11
TRUST

While music is the sound, and dance is what is seen in the conversation, trust is what is sensed. Trust is about what your relationship feels like and is another aspect of partnership.

A few years ago, Lucia had some neurological problems in her leg. She went through a series of tests before she got a diagnosis that she would need surgery. The operation could have compromised her mobility, so she was recommended to the best neurosurgeon in Italy. When Lucia met him, he seemed confident, explaining the reasons behind the diagnosis and the pros and cons of the surgery. It was entirely her decision whether to have the surgery at all and whether to choose him. He knew his stuff and demonstrated competence in several ways, including having a global reputation for achieving great results. Her decision to go for the surgery was not just based on the doctor's reputation and credibility but also about how she felt about him. She trusted him.

Stephen Covey describes trust as a combination of credibility and behaviour. He names four key elements of credibility.[1] Two are about competence. This is what we do: capability and results. Lucia made the appointment because of the doctor's competence. It was how she experienced him that led her to trust him to do the operation.

People who choose to explore coaching with you arrive trusting your competence: your reputation, biography, qualifications and

---

[1] Covey (2006)

experience. When they met, Lucia did not need the surgeon to tell her more about his credentials and his reputation. She needed to feel that she could trust him. Like the surgeon, your credentials and results won't build more trust once you are in the room.

As soon as you are in conversation, people will sense whether they can trust you through how they experience your behaviour. Trust comes through the balance of competence and humanity. Covey's other elements of credibility are integrity and intent. These include being transparent, humble, having no hidden agenda, demonstrating courage and positive intent. They are all about being human.

WHY TRUST MATTERS

Covey talks about how behaviour builds trust over time through:

- talking straight – saying what you see;
- respect – demonstrating that you believe they can do the work;
- clarifying expectations – co-creating the relationship and the work in every session;
- keeping commitments – respecting their time by managing your time well;
- delivering results – getting to their desired outcome;
- practising accountability – checking in.

Taking too long to build more trust before you get down to any work can actually get in the way of useful partnership. Some coaches will take one or two sessions to build trust before they start doing any work. You have trained the thinker that coaching is not about them thinking. Unless you are explicit, *Let's get to know each other before we start the work*, you have implied that you are coaching. You aren't.

When a thinker arrives with low trust, you can quickly demonstrate they can get value out of your time together. This is one of Covey's trust-building behaviours: *delivering results*. Doing some coaching that produces a quick win is a great way to build trust.

IT TAKES TWO TO TRUST

Coaching works best in partnership. You can have all the credibility in the world, but if the thinker doesn't want to think, they won't see results. Trust is a dance. You trust them. They trust you, and you need to trust that when you co-create this conversation in partnership, outcomes will emerge.

At the beginning of the journey, coaches work hard to create a toolbox full of techniques you can use in any situation, thinking it will enhance your competence and credibility. You put pressure on yourself by taking too much responsibility for delivering results, so that you will be seen as reliable and competent. In order to earn trust, there is a belief that you have to demonstrate that you are capable. In fact all you need is enough knowledge and technical skill to believe you can coach. You don't need to know everything!

Who you are in the relationship slowly builds or quickly erodes trust. In John Blakey's nine habits of trust, six are about who you are, not about your competence.[2] They include qualities we have described in Part I: honesty, openness, humility, bravery and kindness.

When you trust someone, you are likely to be trusted in return. Covey believes that trust can be extended. You can only work in partnership with someone when you believe that they are capable of doing good work and that something will change. Psychologist Carl Rogers called this 'unconditional positive regard.'[3] Unconditional is a high bar for humans so perhaps a better description is being as *unconditionally-positive-as-we-are-able-to-be*.

People's life experience and what brought them to coaching with you will all have an impact on how much they trust you or not. Trust is fragile, it 'arrives on foot and leaves on a horseback,' says the Dutch proverb. Those first few minutes matter. When someone

---

[2] Blakey (2016)
[3] Rogers (1957)

arrives for their first conversation with you and says they'd like some advice, you saying *Coaching isn't about giving you any answers* is received as a telling off or an instruction and can slow trust. Getting on with some work and demonstrating that they can come up with their own answers without offering advice will enable them to trust the process and you a little more.

The two scenarios that we encounter the most have very different trust dynamics:

- **Scenario 1 – people who want a coach and find us**
  When we have been recommended to a thinker, or they have heard of us by reputation, trust is part of why they have come. When they arrive, they bring that trust with them. We feel it. There is a different energy. Even when they have not worked with a coach before, there is confidence that they are going to get value out of the session. They trust us and therefore they trust the process, even when they don't know what it is. They are ready to do some work. It is easy to extend or deepen trust from here so that they will make progress even when things get difficult.

- **Scenario 2 – people who are sent to us for coaching**
  When someone is sent to us, probably by their manager or HR, we are in a very different situation. We don't know what they are feeling about being sent, nor whether they know what coaching is, nor whether they think that the coaching is being used as some kind of performance management. They might be reluctant to work with a coach. They might not believe they will get value from it and that we will report back to their manager. We are a long way from having trust in the room unless we ask: *What do we need to talk about so that you trust me enough to do this work?*

If Covey is right that 'trust is the one thing that changes everything', we need to talk about it.[4] We can't work in partnership when we are making the decision alone about whether there is enough trust between us. We need to ask them.

PSYCHOLOGICAL SAFETY

How you begin the relationship and a conversation impacts how much human connection they experience. Co-creating an explicit agreement about confidentiality and clarifying how you will handle the information they share is part of trust and it makes it safer for them to open up. Claire's team sends a confidentiality agreement by email so that people can agree to it before they have their first conversation. This avoids it feeling like the coach is reading the rules in the first few minutes of the encounter. You can talk about anything that they want to add, or clarify, as you begin.

Feeling safe is more than the explicit confidentiality conversation, the logistics, the terms and conditions. 'Your emotions and positive regard have more impact on how safe clients feel than the words you choose,' says coach Marcia Reynolds.[5] Gary Crotaz shared a conversation he had with coach John Baldoni. John works with leaders and is the author of *Grace Under Pressure*. In their conversation, they recognized that there is an implicit contract when you work with people, *We are both agreeing to work with grace, we will trust each other to show respect, we will be open.* Coming together as human people is part of the implicit agreement between you.

They will need to feel safe enough to share their own stuff and trust that what they share will be received by someone who can understand them. As they reveal their story, they will unconsciously assess how it is being received. If they feel dismissed, evaluated, interrupted, talked over (or even noised over with too many *ooh, aah, OK, gotcha*), patronized or insulted, this will impact trust. A listener who is perceived as being judgemental – even when you

---

4 Covey (2006)

5 Reynolds (2020a)

are not – will close the door to deeper work. On the other hand, kindness and empathy, which create a safe space where they feel heard, will allow them to trust you and open up more.

What, then, is safe enough? Feeling heard is critical to a useful conversation and so is the opportunity for the thinker to gain new insights. When you decide that someone needs too much safety, you are demonstrating that you don't trust them to do the work. Blakey and Day describe conversations like this, that are low in challenge and high in support as 'cosy'.[6] Kim Scott calls it 'manipulative insincerity'.[7] You will need to trust that they are robust enough to do some good work. Unless you actively bring enough courage and appropriate vulnerability to demonstrate that trust, you might inadvertently be demonstrating that you don't trust them.

QUESTIONS TO THINK ABOUT

- What do you do to intentionally create safety at the beginning of the relationship?
- What challenges have you encountered around safety?
- How have you overcome them?
- What will you do differently going forward?

TRUST AND EMPATHY

Acknowledging the thinker's emotions with empathy is another important element of how you build trust in the relationship, which impacts the depth of the conversation. Lucia finds it useful to imagine that she is not alone in a conversation with the thinker, recognizing that there are always emotions in the room. Before she starts doing any work, she wonders *Who is in the room with us?* and sometimes will invite them to share what they notice:

---

6 Blakey & Day (2012)
7 Scott (2019)

- What emotions are present for you today?
- How are you feeling in relation to this challenge?
- How is this impacting you as a person?
- And if we go deeper?

Trust has many aspects. Leadership coaches Frances X. Frei and Anne Morriss wrote that 'people tend to trust you when they believe they are interacting with the real you (authenticity), when they have faith in your judgement and competence (logic), and when they feel that you care about them (empathy).'[8] When we talked about vulnerability, we noticed how our human side can become hidden behind the professional. What needs to happen for the real you to be confident enough to show up?

Empathy is one of the qualities of a good coach. Is it useful to feel what others feel? John Blakey talks about kindness and not empathy in his nine habits of trust. Can empathy get us too close to be able to be useful? In *Against Empathy*, psychologist Paul Bloom says that:

> the act of feeling what you think others are feeling – whatever one chooses to call this – is different from being compassionate, from being kind, and most of all from being good. From a moral standpoint, we're better off without it.[9]

Authentic empathy is a good way to connect. Too much empathy can feel overwhelming and can lower trust. Imagine someone sharing a story about multiple challenges at the same time. If you say anything that sounds like 'poor you' you might lose trust straight away. What we like to say instead, *Wow, that's a lot going on for you all at once! What do we need to think about today that could be useful for you?*

---

[8] Frei & Morriss (2020)
[9] Bloom (2016)

QUESTIONS TO THINK ABOUT

- How do you empathize with the people you coach?
- How does your empathy impact distance and trust?
- What needs to be different going forward?

RISK

Transformation and new insight can come when you challenge, and you can only challenge safely when there is enough trust. Blakey and Day describe a *Zone Of Uncomfortable Debate (ZOUD)*. This is where the work happens and where coaches need more than empathy, rapport and respect. This is the place to embrace risk with courage and vulnerability. 'The coach cannot enter the ZOUD if they will not risk breaking rapport. The greatness within a coachee cannot be freed if the coach holds a functioning coachee in a safe place, which in fact cocoons them unnecessarily.'[10] Now is the moment when your trust in them and in the process becomes as important as your trust in yourself and your ability to not know. This is a dance of give and take that embraces every single quality we explored in Part I as we step into the unknown, not knowing whether this challenge will unlock things, or have them lose trust in you.

In a recent supervision, a coach was wondering what to do with a disturbing image that came into her mind as the thinker was doing some somatic work. Claire wondered where it came from. If something happens that is unusual for you, it may be coming from the space between you, or from the thinker. They were in the ZOUD. The coach knew that it would have been unsafe and broken trust if she had shared the image directly with the thinker. And they also wondered whether it was an intuition or feeling that would have added value to the conversation. Entering the ZOUD and keeping safe might look like a gradual offer, asking permission at every stage:

---

[10] Blakey & Day (2012)

Coach:	Can I offer something?
Thinker:	Yes.
Coach:	An image popped up in my mind of [*a gentle description*]
	[*Thinker engages*]
Coach:	May I offer a little more?
Thinker:	Yes.
Coach:	I wonder what sense you make of that?
Coach:	I'm asking myself how this connects with [*something*]?

We can't challenge people unless *we* trust them, believing that they are great people, capable and fully competent. We demonstrate trust through humility and not taking power we do not deserve. We demonstrate trust when we partner from the moment we start throughout the end. When they see us as partners, trust will grow.

QUESTIONS TO THINK ABOUT

- What is your relationship with risk?
- Where have you challenged well lately?
- Where might you need to increase the challenge because you are holding 'a functioning coachee in a safe place'?

PRIVILEGE

How we make people feel when we first meet them is about how we connect and how we both hold our own privilege. This is part of trust-building. Some of the differences and similarities between us will be visible. Some will be invisible. Awareness of our own privilege as human beings is a small step on the journey to arriving in the conversation in our humanity in a way that enables the person we are working with to arrive in theirs.

Microaggressions – where we accidentally say or do something that might feel insensitive or prickly to our companion – 'are not so micro in terms of their impact. They should be taken seriously, because at their core they signal disrespect and reflect inequality.'[11] And they impact how much we trust each other.

We need to make it safe for both of us to acknowledge and talk about differences: *What differences do we need to acknowledge here?* If you are uncomfortable talking about difference, it may be a useful topic to take to supervision.

SIGNS THAT TRUST IS NOT ESTABLISHED ENOUGH

It is not your decision what is enough trust and what is too much. Microaggressions are not the only sign that trust is not enough. You will negotiate safety together if you are not to lead. This negotiation is not something simply for the beginning of a conversation or a relationship. Check in often, every time you meet – enough times for it to be useful and not so many that it is annoying.

Someone arriving for a session disclosed that they had just had a family bereavement. We checked in as we started: *Are you OK to be here today?* and then later in the conversation, *Are you OK to take on some challenge here?* It was the thinker's decision about how safe they felt to go deep as the work progressed. If you are the sole monitor of trust and safety, you may be accidentally disempowering your companion.

In Chapter 1, we talked about someone Claire coached whom she told did not need to disclose their story. They settled into the conversation and began to trust the coaching process once they trusted that their secret was safe. You don't need to know all the intricate details of someone's life. Trusting them to only disclose what is useful to them can be a new experience for people who assume that they have to tell you everything, including things they

---

11 Washington (2022)

would prefer not to share. It is also interesting learning for growing coaches who think they need a lot of context before they can help the thinker.

A final story about trust: Claire was approached by a coach working in an organization where colleagues feared that personal information would be leaked to the press. The coach recognized the value of providing a safe place to ask deep and challenging questions and also knew that trust around the organization was not high enough for them to feel that they could respond honestly. They talked about it and she returned to work ready to ask challenging questions without expecting an answer: *I'm not going to ask you to answer this, but the question I am asking myself is...* This is a practical demonstration of how you can trust someone to do the work themselves. The coaching process does not all have to happen in the room with you.

CHAPTER 12
USING RECORDINGS FOR REFLECTIVE PRACTICE

We have talked about what partnership looks like and sounds like. But how do you know whether you are doing it? What we did and what we think we did in the room are always different. That's why it is useful to sometimes go back, watch, listen and reflect.

WHAT IS REFLECTIVE PRACTICE?

Reflective practice is a great place to work with your own feelings about not being in control and not knowing. Author Gillie Bolton says that:

> Reflective practice helps us accept uncertainty which is the route to effective learning and professional artistry. It enables us to say, 'I don't know what's going on here, and I want to find out.' We find out what kind of practitioner we are. And connect ourselves with our practitioner selves.[1] All this gives confidence and strength to:

- let go of certainty, in a safe enough environment.
- look for direction without knowing where we need to go.
- begin to act without knowing how.[2]

---

[1] Brookfield (1995)

[2] Bolton (2014)

What did I do? What did I hear? What worked? What didn't work? How did they respond? What did I notice? are all useful questions which bring insight. Journalling, one-to-one supervision, action learning sets or supervision groups are great ways of growing as a coach. They rely on what you remember but they don't include how you are really experienced by the thinker. Self-reported data is not enough to evaluate the usefulness or the quality of your coaching. Deep learning cannot be done in the session or through self-reflection alone.

DEEPER LEARNING

What you see, hear and sense enable you to build trust, rapport, listen, form questions and enable the thinker to get in flow. Coaches miss much of what emerges because you have many other things to do, live in the room. What the thinker sees, hears and senses in and from you are equally important. From time to time it's useful learning to pay attention to these. A skilled reflective practitioner new to the idea of recordings said: *I get it! I need to* **adjust me**.

As part of coaches' development, we each spend a couple of days a week with them listening to recordings of their coaching. This is the most impactful way to develop as a coach and a useful way of assessing the competencies of coaching.

This may be the first time you have done a recording; you might not have done one since your training many years ago or you may be wondering why you would need to do one at all. Recordings are useful because they are the only way that you can observe the impact of what you are doing in the room.

Becoming an artful coach requires focus in two areas:

1. Work on your human stuff – this can be seen in the movement and heard in the sound of the conversation.
2. Take the technical coaching skills that you already have, tighten it up and then let it flow.

With a recording, you will learn to appreciate the gaps that need attention to become more artful. You'll notice your strengths as well as your habits. You will learn to watch how your questions and silences land with different thinkers. When coaches use recordings as development, they almost always begin to do less work. And you will start to take less notes! Your conversations will be more in flow. (We will talk about credential applications later in the chapter.)

Video recordings are much better for development than audio, unless you only work on the telephone. You can see the transitional moments of the conversation, the movement that disturbs the flow, what's happening in pauses, who is waiting. You can also notice if something is unsaid.

You might try different approaches to learn from your recordings: individual reflection, debriefing with a peer coach or a mentor coach. If you look at them on your own and you can see, hear or sense what's going on when you are watching the recording, you will probably learn to do that in the room.

Working with a peer is also useful to gain a different perspective. If you are going for ICF credentials, you will have to work with a mentor coach. We recommend that all coaches have mentor coaching to add value to your reflective practice. Mentor coaching 'consists of coaching and feedback in a collaborative, appreciative and dialogued process based on an observed or recorded coaching session to increase the coach's capability in coaching, in alignment with the ICF Core Competencies.'[3]

DO YOU HATE THE SOUND OF YOUR OWN VOICE?

You are not alone. When you speak, you hear what you are saying in two ways, explains BBC science presenter Greg Foot:

> The first is through vibrating sound waves hitting your eardrum, the way other people hear your voice. The second way is through vibrations inside your skull set off by your

---

[3] ICF, *Mentor Coaching*.

vocal cords. Those vibrations travel up through your bony skull and again set the ear drum vibrating. However, as they travel through the bone they spread out and lower in pitch, giving you a false sense of bass.[4]

That is why recordings sound squeaky. This is how you sound to others! You may well cringe, and unless you listen to recordings, you are missing out on some deep learning.

RECORDING FOR DEVELOPMENT

Here are some guidelines to come up with a good recording for your own development.

- **Choose the right thinker**
  - Record what you normally do with people you normally work with, even if it's hybrid coaching (coaching with some mentoring).
  - If there are commercial reasons why you can't record much of your work, you could offer three or four pro bono sessions to people in exchange for a recording.
  - Try to record with someone who is not completely new to coaching: it will take some time for them to go deep.
  - Don't choose someone who is a very experienced coach: they will do all the work by themselves.
  - For learning, a 30-minute session is ideal and a great way of tightening up your coaching.
  - If you aren't yet ready to watch your own recordings, search for coaching demos on YouTube. And watch the thinker. Not the coach.

- **Permissions**
  - You need permission to record. This does not need to be in the recording itself. If you are going to watch the recording with your mentor coach, remember to mention

---

[4] Foot, *Why does your voice sound different on a recording?*

that in your permission request.

- When you ask permission in the recording, or just before you press play, you start one down. You have accidentally told the thinker you are indebted to them! Agreeing in advance by email is clear enough.

- Here is an example of a simple permission request.[5]

  I confirm that I am happy to participate in the recording of my coaching session with :

  Name of Coach

  On (date)

  I understand that:

  - I have agreed to an audio/video recording of my coaching session.

  - My mentor and their supervisor/mentor may review the material in order to monitor and improve my coach's skills.

  - The recording may be uploaded to the International Coaching Federation as part of my coach's accreditation. Only the ICF examiner will hear/watch it.

  - The purpose of the recording is to support my coach's own CPD (continuing professional development).

  - At the end of the session, I have the opportunity to request that the recording is not used.

  - The recording will be deleted within x months unless we agree otherwise.

- If you don't have a data privacy policy (plan), now is the time to sort it out. You will be storing personal information.

- **Getting ready to record**

  - Conquer your recording aversion! While you are worried about recording, you won't be doing what you normally

---

5 You can download this sample from: www.thehumanbehindthecoach.com

do. Get permission to record everything that you can for a while and agree that you will delete them. You might not even watch them. Just get comfortable so that you can begin to record the normal you.

- o If there are any technical challenges during the recording, ignore them and do not apologize for bad internet connection – it is not your fault. Ask them to repeat what they have just said only if you didn't hear at all.
- o Choose lights to make sure your face is visible and not in the dark.
- o Headphones can increase confidentiality because no one else can hear the thinker but if you are using wired headphones remember that they might be an obstacle to movement!
- o Choose a quiet place away from background noise and pick a time of the day when you are less likely to be interrupted.
- o Turn off reminders and notifications on your phone or computer.
- o Record in gallery view so that when you watch back you can see the two of you at the same time. If you are using Zoom this might be on your account settings on the website.
- o Given that it is not normal to see yourself while you are having a conversation live, cover the side of the screen with your picture so you aren't watching yourself! In unrecorded sessions, using *Hide Self View* makes the whole experience more normal.

- **The right mood**
  - o There is no such a thing as a perfect recording.
  - o You will always make mistakes, ask inadequate questions, go too fast or too slow. Only learn as much as is useful to learn from each recording. Over analysing is not going

   to serve you.
- ○ Less is more – listening back to a recording for development every other month will give you time to incorporate new learning in your practice.
- ○ You need to be recording sessions that show you how you do what you do. Please avoid thinking that your mentor coach, supervisor, assessor are also present in the room. It will affect your presence!

- **Watch with someone else**
  - ○ The first time we watch a recording, we watch it with the coach. It's the only way for the coach to get feedback in real time because, like the thinker, we don't know what will happen next. We can only notice what is happening. Watching in advance allows us to give different feedback because we know how the recording will end. They bring deep and different learning.

BE GENTLE

Whether you watch recordings alone or with a peer, mentor or supervisor, looking at too many aspects of your developmental edges could be overwhelming. You will need different kinds of feedback depending on your goal – individual reflection, debrief with a peer or mentor coach, or accreditation. What we offer here are some ideas. Use one or two and make them your own. Over time, it might be useful to be more systematic, but as you begin, please go gently.

Software programmers execute 'debug mode' when a programme is not working properly. Debugging helps find and fix errors. They look at code one line at a time to see its impact on the expected outcome and spot bugs easily. When we mentor very experienced coaches, we might take an hour to look at five minutes of a recording. We pause every time there is something to notice in a sound, a look, a pause and dive deep into the learning. This is not the place to start!

SOME IDEAS

Here are some different ways to watch and listen. Please don't look for them all on your first recording, and please don't try and apply all the learning in your next coaching session. They are simply different lenses:

1. Simply watch the thinker

Tünde Erdös said that 'presence is not about what the coach is doing. It's about the relationship between the coach and the thinker.'[6] Begin by only watching the thinker.
Ask yourself:

- Are they thinking?
- What do you notice when they are thinking? What do you notice when you're unsure whether they are thinking?
- When you spoke, was the thinker ready for you? Or were they busy?

This is the place to learn about silence and timing. You begin to see how the value to the thinker comes from the work they do and just not the words you speak.

2. Do we know what we are doing today?

Watch a recording and notice:

- Who dived into the stuff first? (Any exploring or curious question about the content?)
- Are you *both* clear enough about what you're doing in this session? How you're both going to do it and how you'll know you've done it before *you* dived into exploring?
- Notice the transition points where you change direction. Who made the decision?

---

[6] Erdös (2021a)

- How do you both know that you're still in partnership?
- How often are you checking in? When might you have checked in more?
- Can you clearly see the arc of the coaching container – the beginning, the middle and the end of the conversation?

3. What am I doing and what is happening between us?

When they are looking at you they are probably talking to you. When they begin to look away it is often a sign that they are now thinking for themselves:

- What are you noticing?
- Are you moving forwards or backwards?
- Who is benefitting from the coach's interventions?
- How much is the coach controlling the direction of the conversation?
- How much is the coach rewording questions to make sure they are perfectly formed?
- What happens to the coach when things get difficult and the thinker is stuck?
- How comfortable is the coach when things get difficult?
- What emotions is the coach displaying accidentally?
- What do you see, hear or sense, and how and when are you offering that back?
- As you watch yourself ask a question, notice their eyes – did you stop talking as soon as they picked it up? Were they waiting for you to stop speaking?
- How many questions did you ask in the middle? How many of those questions kept them thinking?
- Who breaks the silences?
- Is your preference feeling or thinking and is their preference feeling or thinking? Are you noticing or offering back both?
- Who is leading? Who is following?

- How much is the conversation in flow? Or is it like table tennis?
- Can you see the transformation emerging?
- Who manages the ending? Are you leading it? Or is it in partnership?

4. The human lens

Reflect on one of the human qualities from Part I:

- When are you demonstrating it and how?
- When are you not demonstrating it?
- What is the impact on the thinker?
- What needs to be different?

There are more reflection opportunities and specific exercises in each chapter.

5. Sound and movement

- Do your questions sound like an offer or a statement? What's the impact?
- What is your *I-hear-you* sound? Does it encourage flow?
- What is your *Go-on-then* noise? Is it an offer or a blocker?
- Are you noticing and saying what you see/hear, e.g. the noises they make, and the laugh?
- What do you see/hear as an insight emerging in them?
- What do you do when they have had an insight? What sound or movement do you notice in them? And what do they notice in you?
- How could you bring more flow and humanity in the rightsizing?
- Are you asking permission before you go to another level? *How deep do you want to go?*

Deeper and different learning can come when you listen with video off or watch with sound off. As you get more confident with using recordings, you will begin to notice where you need to do some of the inside work. What's the one thing you will start with?

And as you watch recordings, if you are coming up with a list of questions you'd like to ask, they may well be the questions you need to start asking the thinker!

TRANSCRIPTS

Looking at the words you actually said in a conversation is an excellent way of addressing bad habits fast! You can see how much you actually talk, rather than how much you think you talk. You can see when you ask multiple questions or offer unsolicited advice. In fact, you can look at a transcript through many lenses and get all kinds of insights and learning about what you need to do more of and what you can do less of in service of facilitating someone else to think. Recording transcripts are a great way for a mentor to see how your questions are structured. There are many low-cost websites where you can upload recordings and get a transcript, e.g. Otter.ai, and Temi.com, Google Meet and Zoom have a free transcript function. Whichever you choose, ensure that your recordings and transcripts are stored safely according to your countries data protection regulations.

USING RECORDINGS FOR ACCREDITATION

Recording is required as part of the credential process for some professional bodies. ICF, for example, requires one or two recordings that demonstrate their coaching competencies.

We recommend that you don't take the first recording you have ever done and analyse it all through the lens of all the ICF competencies. Look at one competency at a time. Reflecting on the questions and observations you raise with your mentor coach will naturally strengthen your coaching competencies, as long as it's not a tick box activity to make sure that you pass a training assessment.

Here are some guidelines to create a recording for assessment with ICF.

- The coaching session must be with someone who has hired you as a coach and not in any other capacity.
- It must last 20–60 minutes.
- They could be a paid or pro bono client.
- The recording must be audio only with a full transcript, including exclamations and other noises. Please refer to the ICF requirements to understand what is needed.
- Ask written permission.

AFTERWORD

We are writing as AI is beginning to be used to coach. Many coaches are sharing their concerns about the future of our profession. We have the technical skills. And our humanity, our sensory and emotional experience, our intuition and our whole selves are what we as humans uniquely bring to coaching.

Let's leave the final words to Sam Isaacson, author of *How to Thrive as a Coach in a Digital World*:

> Our gift to the world can be in the human connection we build with [people]. Technology can provide miraculous ways to achieve just that – how else could we tangibly share moments of deep connection with someone on the other side of the world…? Let's double down on our commitment to being the best coaches we can be, bringing a deeper sort of magic to the world than any machine ever will.[1]

As you finish the book, what one quality will make the biggest difference moving forward?

---

[1] Isaacson (2021)

BIBLIOGRAPHY

3D Coaching. *Efforting.* October 2022. Available from: https://www.3dcoaching.com/blog/3d-ideas-1012-efforting [accessed March 2023].

Ackerman, Courtney E. 'What is Self-Worth and How Do We Build It?', Positive Psychology. 2018. Available from: https://positivepsychology.com/self-worth [accessed March 2023].

Adamson, Fiona and Brendgen, Jane. *Mindfulness-Based Relational Supervision.* Routledge: 2022.

Anderson, Carly. *Partnering – The Approach that Differentiates Coaching from Other Professions.* 2015. Available from: https://carlyanderson.com/partnering-the-approach-that-differentiates-coaching-from-other-professions

Angelou, Maya. 'Race, Morality and Lessons to a Daughter', *Bill Moyers Journal.* 2023. Available from: https://vimeo.com/96767082?embedded=true&source=video_title&owner=9013478

Baldelli, Lucia. *Coaching Outside the Box.* 2023. Available from: www.coachingoutsidethebox.net/intuition-vs-interpretation/ [accessed March 2023].

Blakey, John. *The Trusted Executive.* Kogan Page: 2016.

Blakey, John and Day, Ian. *Challenging Coaching*. Nicholas Brealey Publishing: 2012.

Bloom, Paul. *Against Empathy*. Penguin Random House: 2016.

Bolton, Gillie. *Reflective Practice*. Sage: 2014.

Botsman, Rachel Does humility undermine credibility? Available from: www.linkedin.com/pulse/humility-success-rachel-botsman [accessed March 2023]

Botsman, Rachel. *Who Can You Trust?* Penguin: 2018.

Botsman, Rachel. ICF Converge Conference (keynote speech), 2021.

Brackett, Marc. *Permission to Feel*. Celadon Books: 2019.

Bradley, Alistair. 'An Empirical Exploration into Changes Coaches Perceive Associated with Experience of Flow in Coaching Conversations', Thesis Paper, 2022. Available from: https://doi.org/10.24384/wtzr-de77 [accessed April 2023].

Brann, Amy. *Neuroscience for Coaches*. Kogan Page: 2022.

Brookfield, Stephen D. *Becoming a Critically Reflective Teacher*. Jossey-Bass: 1995.

Brown, Brené. *Atlas of the Heart*. Vermillion: 2021.

Brown, Brené. *Dare to Lead*. Vermillion: 2018.

Brown, Brené. *Daring Greatly*. Penguin Life: 2015a.

Brown, Brené. *Rising Strong*. Vermillion: 2015b.

Brown, Brené. *The Gifts of Imperfection*. Vermillion: 2020.

Brown, Brené. *The Power of Vulnerability*. Audiobook Sounds True: 2012.

Bungay Stanier, Michael. *The Advice Trap*. Page Two: 2020.

Cardon, Alain. *L'art véritable du maître coach – Un savoir être au service de l'émergence*. InterEditions: 2011.

Carey, Dr Timothy A. *The Being of Humans*. October 2016. Available from: www.psychologytoday.com/us/blog/in-control/201510/the-being-humans [accessed April 2023].

Carter, Martin. LinkedIn post. 2022. Available from: www.linkedin.com/feed/update/urn:li:activity:6907956186742956032 [accessed February 2023].

Clance, Pauline R. and Imes, Suzanne. 'The Imposter Phenomenon in High Achieving Women: Dynamics and Therapeutic Intervention', *Psychotherapy: Theory, Research & Practice,* 15(3): 241–247, 1978. Available from: https://doi.org/10.1037/h0086006

Clutterbuck, David. 'The Liberated Coach', *Coaching: An International Journal of Theory Research and Practice,* (2): 73–81, March 2010.

Copp, Trevor and Fox, Jeff. *Liquid Lead Dancing – It Takes Two to Lead*. Available from: https://youtu.be/OH0dK208MNk [accessed March 2023].

Covey, Stephen. *The Speed of Trust*. Simon & Schuster: 2006.

Crotaz, Gary. *The Unlock Moment*. 2022. Available from: https://theunlockmoment.com/2022/03/17/the-unlock-moment-micahlorenc-you-dont-always-have-to-play-safe/ [accessed February 2023].

Damon, William. *The Path to Purpose*. Free Press: 2009.

David, Susan. *Emotional Agility*. Penguin: 2017.

Dutton, Jane. *Energize Your Workplace: How to Create and Sustain High-Quality Connections at Work*. Jossey-Bass: 2003.

Eggert, Max. *Brilliant Body Language*. Pearson Education: 2010.

Einzig, Hetty. *The Future of Coaching*. Routledge: 2017.

Eliot, Thomas, E. *Four Quartets – Burnt Norton*. Faber & Faber: 1974.

Erdös, Tünde. 'Being Human' in *The Coaching Inn* podcast. 2021a. Available from: https://thecoachinginn.podbean.com/e/in-conversation-with-tunde-erdos-being-human [accessed March 23].

Erdös, Tünde. *Coaching Presence*. Open University Press: 2021b.

Evans, Pippa. *Improv Your Life*. Hodder Studio: 2021.

Foot, Greg. *Why does your voice sound different on a recording?* Available from: https://youtu.be/why-does-your-voice-sound-different-on-a-recording [accessed March 2023].

Franklin, Marilyn. *The Heart of Laser-Focused Coaching*. Thomas Noble: 2019.

Frei, Frances X. and Morriss, Anne. 'Begin with Trust', *Harvard Business Review:* May–June 2020.

Friedman, Edwin. *A Failure of Nerve: Leadership in the Age of the Quick Fix*. Seabury Books: 2007.

Giles, Howard; Coupland, Nikolas and Coupland, Justine. *Contexts of Accommodation*. Cambridge University Press: 1991.

Gladwell, Malcolm. *Blink: The Power of Thinking Without Thinking*. Little, Brown & Company: 2005.

Gordon, Amie M. 'The Role of Familiarity in Attraction', *Psychology Today*. 2022. Available from: www.psychologytoday.com/us/blog/between-you-and-me/202203/the-role-familiarity-in-attraction [accessed March 2023]

Grant, Adam. *Think Again.* Penguin Random House: 2021.

Gravois, John. 'You're Not Fooling Anyone', *The Chronicle of Higher Education*, 54(11): A1, 2007.

Green, Charles. *The Trusted Advisor Fieldbook*. Wiley: 2011.

Hawkins, Peter and Turner, Eve. *Systemic Coaching: Delivering Value Beyond the Individual*. Routledge: 2019.

Hemphill, Prentis. Instagram. Available from: www.instagram.com/prentishemphill

Hess, Edward and Ludwig, Katherine. *Humility Is the New Smart: Rethinking Human Excellence in the Smart Machine Age*. Berrett-Koehler Publishers: 2017.

Holmes, Chris. *The Secret Sauce in Coaching*. International Coaching Federation. 2020. Available from: https://coachingfederation.org/blog/the-secret-sauce-in-coaching [accessed March 2023]

Hope Hailey, Prof V. 'Leadership through COVID-19: How has the Pandemic Changed Leadership for the Future?', *CIPD*. 2021. Available from: www.cipd.co.uk/news-views/changing-work-views/future-work/thought-pieces/leadership-through-covid#grief [accessed May 2023]

Infante, Dominic; Rancer, Andrew S. and Avtgis, Theodore A. *Contemporary Communication Theory*. Kendall Hunt Publishing: 2009.

International Coaching Federation (ICF). *Mentor Coaching*. Available from: https://coachingfederation.org/credentials-and-standards/mentor-coaching [accessed March 2023].

International Coaching Federation (ICF). *Updated ICF Core Competencies*. 2019. Available from: https://coachingfederation.org/app/uploads/2021/03/ICF-Core-Competencies-updated.pdf

Isaacs, William. *Dialogue*. Bantam Doubleday Dell Publishing Group: 1999.

Isaacson, Sam. *How to Thrive as a Coach in a Digital World*. Open University Press: 2021.

Jourard, Sidney M. *The Transparent Self*. D. Van Norstand Company, Inc.: 1972.

Kline, Nancy. *The Promise that Changes Everything*. Penguin Life: 2020.

Kline, Nancy. *Time to Think*. Cassell: 2002.

Klotz, Kelsey. *The Art of the Mistake*. 2017. Available from: https://commonreader.wustl.edu/c/the-art-of-the-mistake [accessed March 2023]

Knowles, Josephine, 'Let's Talk – Power and the Dance of Coaching' in *The Coaching Inn* podcast. 2021. https://thecoachinginn.podbean.com/e/let-s-talk-josephine-knowles [accessed March 2023].

Lambert, Shaun. *A Book of Sparks: A Study in Christian Mindfullness.* Instant Apostle: 2014.

Machiavelli, Niccolò. In a letter to Lorenzo de' Medici written in 1516 to dedicate his book *The Prince.* Available from: https://letteritaliana.weebly.com/la-lettera-dedicatoria.html [accessed March 2023].

Maister, David H.; Galford, Robert and Green, Charles. *The Trusted Advisor: 20th Anniversary Edition.* Free Press, Anniversary Edition: 2021.

Mannix, Kathryn. *Listen: How to Find the Words for Tender Conversations.* William Collins: 2021.

Maté, Gabor. *When the Body Says No.* Wiley: 2011.

Maxwell, John. *Thinking for a Change: 11 Ways Highly Successful People Approach Life and Work.* Center Street: 2003.

McGill, Bryant. *Voice of Reason.* Paper Lyon Publishing: 2012.

Moby. *Moby Discusses his Issues.* April 2009. Available from: www.interviewmagazine.com/art/moby-issue-project-room [accessed February 2023].

Morrison, Lennox. *Worklife,* BBC. 2017. Available from: www.bbc.com/worklife/article/20170718-the-subtle-power-of-uncomfortable-silences [accessed February 2023].

Neff, Kristin. *Self-Compassion*. Hodder & Stoughton: 2011.

O'Donohue, John. *Conamara Blues*. Bantam: 2001.

Pedrick, Claire. *Simplifying Coaching*. Open University Press: 2020.

Pilhofer, Michael and Day, Holly. *Music for Dummies*. For Dummies: 2019.

Potok, Chaim. *The Chosen*. Penguin: 2009.

Potter, Stephen. *One-upmanship: Being Some Account of the Activities and Teaching of the Lifemanship Correspondence College of One-Upness and Gameslifemastery*. Penguin: 1962. (First Edition, Rupert Hart-Davis, 1952).

Price, Colin and Toye, Sharon. *Accelerating Performance: How Organizations Can Mobilize, Execute, and Transform with Agility*. Wiley: 2017.

Reynolds, Marcia. *Coach the Person, not the Problem*. Berrett-Koehler Publishers: 2020a.

Reynolds, Marcia. *The Key to Effective Coaching: Psychologically Safe Partnering that Encourages Discomfort*. May 2020b. Available from: https://trainingindustry.com/articles/leadership/the-key-to-effective-coaching-psychologically-safe-partnering-that-encourages-discomfort [accessed April 2023].

Rock, Dr. David. *Your Brain at Work*. Harper Business: 2020.

Rock, David and Schwarz, Jeffrey. 'The Neuroscience of Leadership', *Strategy + business*. 30 May 2006. Available from: www.strategy-business.com/article/06207 [accessed July 2023].

Rogers, Carl R. 'The Necessary and Sufficient Conditions of Therapeutic Personality Change', *Journal of Consulting Psychology*, 21(2): 95–103, 1957.

Rohr, Richard. *Falling Upward.* Wiley: 2011.

Sakulku, Jaruwan and Alexander, James. 'The Impostor Phenomenon', *The Journal of Behavioral Science*, 6(1): 75–97, 2011. https://doi.org/10.14456/ijbs.2011.6

Schein, Edgar. *Helping.* Berrett-Koehler Publishers: 2009.

Schein, Edgar. *Humble Inquiry.* Berrett-Koehler Publishers: 2013.

Scott, Kim. *Radical Candor.* Pan: 2019. Available from: www.radicalcandor.com/our-approach [accessed March 2023].

Seiler, Hélène. *Using Client Feedback in Executive Coaching.* Open University Press: 2021.

Shapiro, Lawrence and Spaulding, Shannon. 'Embodied Cognition', *Stanford Encyclopedia of Philosophy (Fall Edition)*, Edward N. Zalta (ed.). 2021. https://plato.stanford.edu/entries/embodied-cognition [accessed June 2023].

Silsbee, Doug. *Presence-Based Coaching: Cultivating Self-Generative Leaders Through Mind, Body, and Heart.* Jossey-Bass: 2008.

Stietz, Julia; Jauk, Emanuel; Krach, Sören and Kanske, Philipp. 'Dissociating Empathy from Perspective-Taking: Evidence from Intra- and Inter-Individual Differences Research Frontiers', *Psychiatry*, 10: 126, 2019.

Stone Zander, Rosamund and Zander, Benjamin. *The Art of Possibility: Transforming Professional and Personal Life.* Penguin: 2006.

Sylvester, Steven. *Detox Your Ego*. Headline: 2016.

Tashiro, Ty. *The Science of Why We're Socially Awkward and Why That's Awesome*. William Morrow: 2017.

Tashiro, Ty. *TED Talks*. Available from: https://youtu.be/WRCwlCo89LU [accessed February 2023].

The Hideout Theatre. Available from: www.hideouttheatre.com/about/what-is-improv [accessed March 2023].

The Killers. 2018. Available from: https://nowordsnosong.medium.com/human-the-killers-678b126468d [accessed November 2022].

Walker, Simon. *The Undefended Leader*. Piquant Editions: 2010.

Washington, Ella F. *Recognizing and Responding to Microaggressions at Work*. 2022. Available from: https://hbr.org/2022/05/recognizing-and-responding-to-microaggressions-at-work [accessed March 2023].

Waytz, Adam. 'The Psychology of Social Status', *Scientific American*. 2009. Available from: www.scientificamerican.com/article/the-psychology-of-social

Weber, Max. 'The Three Types of Legitimate Rule', *Berkeley Publications in Society and Institutions*, 4(1): 1–11. Translated by Hans Gerth, 1958.

Weick, Karl E.; Sutcliffe, Kathleen M. and Obstfeld, David. 'Organizing and the Process of Sensemaking', *Organization Science*, 16(4): 409–421, 2005.

Weiser Cornell, Ann. *Focusing Tip #792 – Felt Sensing Versus Intuition*. Available from: https://focusingresources.com/2022/04/06/

focusing-tip-792-felt-sensing-versus-intuition [accessed March 2023].

Whittington, John. *Systemic Coaching and Constellations*. Kogan Page: 2020.

Zak, Paul. 'How our Brains Decide When to Trust', *Harvard Business Review:* 18 July 2019.

Zornek, Beatrice. LinkedIn post. Available from: https://uk.linkedin.com/in/beatrice-zornek [accessed March 2023].

INDEX

www.ingramcontent.com/pod-product-compliance
Lightning Source LLC
Chambersburg PA
CBHW061337250726
48657CB00004B/1212